MODEST A

— and —

MODERN FASHION

---

*A Biblical examination of modesty and
the modern fashion culture*

D. LOWDEN

ISBN - 978-0-9556218-8-8

Book designed and printed by
Vision Solutions NI
2 Clara Street
Belfast
Northern Ireland
BT5 5GB

ACKNOWLEDGMENTS

My sincere and grateful thanks are due to the following:

My family, for their love and support.

My grandfather, Mr. Noel Lowden, for his help and counsel.

Pastor Ian Wilson, for his help and counsel.

Mr. Simon A. Hailes, for his friendship, for lending and obtaining me many books, and for proof reading the final manuscript.

Mr. Stephen Hogg of Vision Solutions N.I., for all of his help and professional advice in producing this book.

All Scripture quotations are taken only from the Authorised (King James) Version of the Holy Bible.

In recent years I have met many sincere and godly Christians in evangelical churches and gatherings under many different names. I wish to assure the reader therefore, that any reference to a church or assembly of God's people in this book is not an attack on any particular denomination or group of Christians, but rather a general observation of a particular problem that is so widespread that it cannot be ignored, either in society or in the church of Jesus Christ.

I acknowledge my own guilt before God for succumbing to the wiles of the devil in the realm of fashion in the past, and trust that this book will be used of God to the glory of our Lord Jesus Christ.

"...that ye should earnestly contend for the faith which was once delivered unto the saints." - Jude 3

Daniel Lowden
2011

CONTENTS

INTRODUCTION

Laying a Biblical foundation

> *"I beseech you therefore, brethren, by the mercies of God, that ye present your bodies a living sacrifice, holy, acceptable unto God, which is your reasonable service. And be not conformed to this world: but be ye transformed by the renewing of your mind, that ye may prove what is that good, and acceptable, and perfect, will of God."*
>
> *Romans 12:1-2*

This well-known and often quoted passage of Scripture, which follows eleven chapters of salvation truth, summarizes the basics of the Christian life. Having been saved, the Christian is to present his body a living sacrifice, and this sacrifice is to be holy, and acceptable unto God. And not only is the Christian's body to be presented unto God in this manner, but the Christian *himself* or *herself* is not to be conformed to the world. Instead, he or she is to be transformed by the renewing of their mind.

This may seem like an unnecessary repetition of the above passage, but it is essential to take a closer look at the words of these verses, because they show us what a high standard of holy Christian living God requires of His servants. It is our 'reasonable service.' This means that it is to be reasonably expected of us. And it is only by doing this, that we fulfill the will of God, that is described here as 'good, acceptable, and perfect.'

If our bodies, therefore, are to be presented to God, holy and acceptable to Him for His use, then it follows that this should include the whole area of dress and clothing. Some may argue that because *"man looketh on the outward appearance, but the Lord looketh on the heart"* (1 Samuel 16:7b), then the whole realm of clothing is unimportant to God, provided a person's heart is right. But this is untrue. And to interpret this verse in such a way is to misuse it. In 1 Samuel chapter 16, when God was guiding Samuel to choose a king for Israel, He instructed him, *"...look not on his countenance, or on the height of his stature; because I have refused him..."* (1 Samuel 16:7). The context was the man's physical appearance and strength, not his clothing. Elsewhere, however, throughout Scripture, God has very much indeed to say about clothing. The second part of that same verse, (1 Samuel 16:7), tells us: *"...for the LORD seeth not as man seeth; for man looketh on the outward appearance, but the LORD looketh on the heart."*

This tells us that **man indeed looks on the outward appearance.**

Therefore, for believers, the outward appearance is important because we belong to Jesus Christ. And the world should recognize by our appearance that we belong to Jesus Christ, because we are not to be conformed to the world. If our hearts are fully yielded to the will of God, then our outward appearance should not contradict this, because, **although God looks upon the heart, men do not see our hearts.** What they see, initially, is our outward appearance.

From Genesis to Revelation, God's standards for dress are clearly revealed, and are given great importance. And if we are to to present our bodies a living sacrifice, holy, and acceptable unto God, then the clothing on our bodies should be acceptable unto Him also. And if we are not to be conformed to the world, then we should not be conformed to the world's standards of dress. Rather, we should follow God's standards.

Personal Testimony

The whole subject of dress, appearance, and worldly fashion has been an enormous personal challenge to the writer. I am greatly ashamed, as I have undertaken this project, to remember the former lusts of my ignorance which God in His great mercy delivered me from. Having had the privilege of being raised in a Christian home, I was converted to faith in Jesus Christ at the age of four. As a teenager, growing up in a Christian Fellowship Church, I mixed with young professing Christian adults who were friendly and sociable, but whose behaviour and lifestyles were rebellious and ungodly. A disregard for any standards of holiness in Christian living was the order of the day. I witnessed activities such as late-night parties where 18-rated movies were watched and alcohol was consumed, swearing and coarse joking (sometimes on the church premises), playing rock music with obscene lyrics, and, at a summer youth camp, promiscuous behaviour and drug abuse. One can imagine the destructive influence this had upon a young Christian teenager. However, I must bear responsibility for my own sin.

Influenced by a carnal desire for popularity, as a young man I also became a very worldly, 'carnal Christian', believing that one could still live as a Christian and enjoy some of what the world had to offer, within certain boundaries. I proceeded to engage in the pursuit of worldly pleasure with several other young adults from the same church. This included attending public bars and nightclubs, addiction to secular rock music, and ungodly behaviour. I was still a professing Christian to most people who knew me, and tried to avoid any activity which I considered to be overtly sinful. This, however, was hypocrisy; an attempt to justify an ungodly love for the world. The church of my upbringing, which practiced love and good works but did not preach a clear gospel message or any Biblical standards of holiness, failed to address such behaviour among young people. Worldliness was rarely preached against or reproved from Scripture. We were not accountable to anyone. In fact, some of the older members occasionally joined us in our social activities.

I continued to attend most of the church services, was involved in church activities, had regular 'quiet times', and tried to maintain some form of Christian testimony, albeit a very weak one. I was a friend of the world, which is condemned by Scripture (James 4, v.4). I lived with 'one foot in the world and one foot in the church'. My times of prayer were usually an attempt to clear a guilty conscience before God. I attempted to increase my 'service' to Christ. After moving to another town I was a youth leader in a small Christian Fellowship there for several years. I later became a member of another small church. Meanwhile, I was a worldly, covetous and foolish young man; a mere 'professor' of Christianity. This was the result of a divided heart, a heart that partly loved Christ and partly loved the world. I was not alone in this, as most of my Christian peers and friends led similar lifestyles.

This continued for approximately seven years until my grandfather began to invite me to meetings in his local Gospel Hall. He had been an elder in this particular assembly for many years, and continues to serve there today. I

4

believe that this was the providence and mercy of God, because the preaching that I heard during those meetings, and the godly, humble manner of the believers whom I met there, had a profound influence upon me. During this time I came under deep conviction of sin. In 2003, at the age of 26, by God's grace, I repented of my worldly lifestyle, backsliding and hypocrisy and sought God's forgiveness for my sin. One evening that same year, for the first time in my Christian experience, I fell to my knees by my bedside, and surrendered my will completely to Christ.

There was still, however, much transformation work to be carried out by the Lord. Even when I enrolled as a Bible college student that same year, I had a great deal of learning to do. Although I had given up the former worldly activities, there were still attitudes of worldliness and carnality in my heart that the Holy Spirit convicted me of, as I studied the Scriptures and sought His will for my life.

I wish to emphasise, at this point, that I am not advocating an unscriptural doctrine of sinless perfection. 1 John 1:8 tells us: *"If we say that we have no sin, we deceive ourselves, and the truth is not in us."* I do, however, believe that holiness in every single aspect of our Christian lives is a fundamental doctrine of the faith. The following scripture has been a tremendous rebuke and challenge to me in recent times:

> *"Having therefore these promises, dearly beloved, let us cleanse ourselves from all filthiness of the flesh and spirit, perfecting holiness in the fear of God."*
>
> *2 Corinthians 7:1*

For many years I had been deceived by the contemporary Christian philosophy that one can be a Christian and still be 'cool'. It is assumed by many today that in order to reach the world for Christ, we need to be 'relevant' to the culture in which we live. This modern way of thinking is promoted by prominent leaders of the so-called 'Emerging Church' movement. Mark Driscoll, pastor of Mars Hill Church, Seattle, USA, has described himself as 'theologically conservative' and 'culturally liberal'. Although Driscoll is a hugely influential preacher who has regular doctrinal teaching sessions in his church, and has even disassociated himself from some very liberal 'emerging church' leaders (such as Rob Bell and Brian McClaren who deny the existence of a literal hell), it is a documented fact that the Mars Hill church engages in many ungodly activities in order to be relevant to the culture of the day. These include secular rock concerts, New Year's Eve 'champagne' parties, men's meetings in which 'R' rated movies are watched and discussed, men's poker nights, and other similar activities.

It is a documented fact that on some occasions (Driscoll himself having admitted this), groups of young people walked out of auditoriums during Driscoll's teaching sessions, because some of his descriptions of sexual matters were so pornographic in their nature that the young people were grossly offended. One such example, for which he has become infamous, is a vile, blasphemous and pornographic interpretation of the Old Testament book *Song of Solomon.* It is now a well-known fact that this damnable 'emerging church' philosophy is spreading itself throughout the evangelical world. According to the Bible, however, friendship with the world is enmity with God:

> ***"Ye adulterers and adulteresses, know ye not that the friendship of the world is enmity with God? Whosoever therefore will be a friend of the world is the enemy of God."***
>
> *James 4:4*

"Love not the world, neither the things that are in the world. If any man love the world, the love of the Father is not in him. For all that is the world, the lust of the flesh, and the lust of the eyes, and the pride of life, is not of the Father, but is of the world. And the world passeth away, and the lust thereof: but he that doeth the will of God abideth forever."

1 John 2:15-17

When I first encountered these Scriptures, I had no peace from God until I repented of my own sinful worldliness. One of the most difficult areas of my life that I believe the Holy Spirit convicted me of, was the whole subject of worldly fashion. For some years, my manner of dress and appearance was, at times, utterly shameful. A large percentage of my income was squandered on gaudy, ill-fitting 'designer' style clothes for men. At one stage, my appearance became so vain and effeminate that it resembled the fashions of homosexuality. And it was the result of a heart that was full of vanity and pride. But thanks to the grace of God, and the conviction of the Holy Spirit through the Word of God, He has led me to repentance. I am now convinced that there is absolutely no place for vanity or worldliness in the life of the Christian, and this must be evident by his or her manner of dress.

Aim of this book

I t is for the reasons already outlined that I am burdened to help and warn others, particularly young people, but also adults, of the wickedness and corruption that permeates the world of fashion. If ever there were a time when the neglected Biblical principles of modesty and gender distinction needed to be sounded forth like a trumpet, I believe it is today. It is not my desire or intention to cause offence to any Christian brother or sister. However, some Christian women may be offended later when I mention certain specific items of clothing which I am convinced, according to the Bible's standards, are not modest. I wish to assure the reader that everything contained in this book is written in love. I wish to help Christian sisters to avoid causing men to stumble, and to honour Christ with their clothing. Some Christian men, who are my brethren in Christ, may also be displeased by my mentioning some items of clothing which may be worn by their own wives and daughters. I certainly do not intend to trespass upon their authority as the individual heads of their homes, but merely wish to help them see what I have seen in the Scriptures.

Some may argue that in matters such as food and drink, God's Word allows liberty and personal choice in these areas; therefore the same principle should apply to matters of dress and clothing. That may be true, but only as far as God's Word permits. There are limitations, and the Word of God makes clear what these limitations are. For example, we are not to cause other believers to stumble or to be offended by those personal choices that we make:

"It is good neither to eat flesh, nor to drink wine, NOR ANYTHING WHEREBY THY BROTHER STUMBLETH, OR IS OFFENDED, OR IS MADE WEAK."

Romans 14:21

Again, with regard to the Christian woman's clothing; the woman has the privilege of a certain amount of personal choice (with reference to her husband if she is married) *but, her manner of dress must be MODEST,* because this is clearly commanded in Scripture, in 1 Timothy 2:9-10. We will be examining this and other passages of Scripture in detail later, and we shall see that modesty is not a matter of mere external reformation. It is a matter of the heart. If the Christian woman's heart is devoted entirely to Jesus Christ, then her outward conduct and appearance should entirely reflect this.

It must be acknowledged that a very large proportion of fashion clothing available to young (and older) women today could not be described as 'modest'. I believe that it would be unfair, therefore, to lay all the blame for the immodesty of today's society at the door of young women themselves. The fashion industry is corrupt to the core with lust and perversion. It is therefore equally guilty for peddling its' shameful products to the retail markets and high street stores, and for seducing impressionable young women from a very early age to dress in the most sensual and provocative fashions.

Some dramatic changes have occurred over the last century, with the evil influence of the Hollywood film industry, rock and pop music, and the social revolution of the 1960s, to name but just a few factors. In addition to this, the profanity and obscenity of modern television programmes such as *X Factor, Strictly Come Dancing, Friends, Sex in the City,* and the filthiness of

9

wicked pop stars such as *Madonna, Lady Ga Ga, Christina Aguilera,* and others, have contributed their corrupting influence because of their sheer popularity, even among professing Christians. I do not own a television, and so thankfully have not witnessed any of the latest lewd performances by these artists. However, I have heard sufficient evidence from common reports on radio articles and other sources to know that if Christians today had any spiritual discernment, they should utterly reject such influences from their lives and homes. I received a recent report from a brother in Christ concerning the latest music video from one of the above mentioned female pop artists, the details of which I will not print. Suffice to say, that the blasphemy of this individual's video performance is so vile and damnable that I could not bear to repeat it. How any Christian who claims to fear God could allow such wickedness to cross the threshold of their homes through a television screen, is unthinkable. It is frightening to consider that such female artists are now regarded as role models for girls and women today, and that Christian families are doing little to protect their children from such evil.

There was a time, little over a hundred years ago, when public decency was a part of everyday society. Feminine modesty, masculine dignity, and a clear distinction between men and women were the standard of most clothing fashions. I am privileged to own several books which contain black and white photographs dating from the turn of the last century which illustrate this fact. One such example is a photograph of Bundoran Beach in County Donegal, in the North of Ireland, dated around 1910. All the men and women on the beach are fully and properly clothed. The men are clothed respectably, in distinctive suits and hats, and the women are clothed modestly, with hats and long, distinctive, loose fitting dresses, and upper garments buttoned to the neck, with nothing exposed. The hats, presumably, were worn to provide protection from the heat and from strong sunlight. But there is absolutely no nakedness or immodesty visible anywhere. If this was the standard on the beach during the summer season, then one can imagine how high the ordinary standard of modesty must have been in other places during other seasons of the year!

Another photograph is of a large group of people standing on the platform of a railway station in Garvagh, County Londonderry, awaiting a train. It is dated from around 1905, and provides remarkable detail. Most of the individuals in the picture are looking towards the camera, and include men, women and children. The author's footnote states that the group is an Edwardian excursion party, on their way to the seaside. All the women are dressed in long, wide, ankle-length skirts, blouses buttoned to the neck, and distinctive hats. The men also are dressed in a conventional, decent manner, with trousers, shirts, ties, waistcoats, watch chains, and hats. It appears that the group includes people from various 'classes' of society at that time. Railway staff and workers are shown standing alongside respectably-dressed passengers. This proves that standards of modesty and decency were generally respected by everyone, regardless of social class or status.

Indeed, other photographs, dating from the same period (around 1900), taken outside railway stations and other locations throughout Ulster and the rest of Ireland, prove that modesty and decency were taken for granted as part of everyday society.

Such is certainly not the case today. Within just a few generations, the very opposite of the above description has become the order of the day. In stark contrast to the careful and modest covering of the body, (even on the beach) at summertime just a century ago, young women today are encouraged to expose as much of their flesh as they can get away with on the streets during summer. The grossly indecent shorts, skirts, swimsuits and other similar items of today are so shocking in their nature when compared to the modest dresses of only a hundred years ago.

Immodesty and indecency are so prevalent in our society now, that many of the current fashions of the day would have been considered the clothing of prostitutes in the past. What could have been described *"the attire of an harlot"* (Proverbs 7:10), several generations ago, is now sold to young women in high street fashion stores. And it has become acceptable in everyday society. Provocative, short, suggestive, tight fitting, revealing styles of clothing are so common upon young women today, that immodesty has been forcibly imposed upon society by the fashion industry. Even Christian women are enticed by the sensual and seductive appeal of modern fashion clothing. In addition to this, we cannot underestimate the influence of lewd, profane, pornographic images on display at every newspaper and magazine stand, and the nudity of advertisements on the rear panels of buses and in the windows of retail fashion stores such as *T.K. Maxx*. One cannot even walk through the *Victoria Square* shopping mall in Belfast without being confronted with larger than life-size images of female models that are almost pornographic in their nature. It is surely no co-incidence that society has become more sexually obsessed, and more morally depraved than ever before in recent generations.

> *"And we know that we are of God, and the whole world lieth in wickedness."*
>
> *1 John 5:19*

Christians are supposed to be engaged in a spiritual warfare (Ephesians 6:11-17). Christian women therefore, have the opportunity, and indeed the responsibility, to resist the *"wiles of the devil"* (Ephesians 6:11) in the world of fashion. Again, *"modest apparel"* is clearly commanded in the Bible (1 Timothy 2:9). Christian women who love their Saviour and seek to serve

Him sincerely with their whole hearts and lives, must determine to 'go against the grain' of this present wicked culture, and choose to please and obey God with modest clothing, rather than conform to the world's standard of clothing.

Likewise, Christian men are engaged in this spiritual warfare. Paul instructed Timothy: *"Thou therefore endure hardness, as a good soldier of Jesus Christ. No man that warreth entangleth himself with the affairs of this life; that he may please him who hath chosen him to be a soldier"* (2 Timothy 2:3-4). Men have the responsibility to please the Lord Jesus Christ by their conduct towards women, their own manner of dress, and also to lead and instruct their families, and this will be examined in the following chapters.

The aim of this book is to examine closely what the Word of God teaches on the subject of the Christian's clothing, and to apply these principles accordingly. There are key passages containing principles that apply both to men and women, however greater attention will be given to the Christian woman's part and the reason for this will become apparent. However, I strongly urge both men and women to read *all* chapters. By reading the chapter *'THE RESPONSIBILITY OF MEN'*, for example, the Christian woman should gain an understanding of how men are affected, visually, by immodest dress styles.

During the course of preparing this study, I have found it necessary to give descriptions of clothing styles which are highly immodest in their nature and design. In doing so, however, I have endeavoured, with the utmost caution, to avoid any vulgar language or inappropriate detail. The Scripture commands us: *"Let no corrupt communication proceed out of your mouth, but that which is good to the use of edifying, that it may minister grace*

unto the hearers" (Ephesians 4:29). I sincerely ask the reader, therefore, to be patient and understanding when they encounter such descriptions later, as I am convinced that it has been necessary to expose the sinfulness of many items of immodest fashion clothing.

> *"And have no fellowship with the unfruitful works of darkness, but rather reprove them. For it is a shame even to speak of those things which are done of them in secret. But all things that are reproved are made manifest by the light: for whatsoever doth make manifest is light. Wherefore he saith, Awake thou that sleepest, and arise from the dead, and Christ shall give thee light. See then that ye walk circumspectly, not as fools, but as wise, redeeming the time, because the days are evil."*
>
> *Ephesians 5:11-16*

I wish to stress, also, that I have not viewed any photograph or image of any of the indecent items of clothing that I have mentioned in this book, or any individual modelling such items, either from the internet, films, television, magazines, books or any other source, as part of my research during the course of this study. Any examples quoted are from memory and common experience. With the exception of the photographs already referred to from the late 1800s and early 1900s, and one consultation to the Wikipedia website to check the spelling of an individual's name, I have consulted absolutely no other secular source. My research for this study has been exclusively Bible based, with occasional reference to other sound Christian materials and literature.

A close examination of key passages from both the Old and New Testaments, will be the basis for this study. It is the writer's absolute conviction that if the believer in Jesus Christ is willing to surrender this relatively simple area of his or her life completely to His will and obey the commandments of Scripture, then blessing will follow, as the Christian presents his or her body a living sacrifice, holy and acceptable unto God.

> *"What? know ye not that your body is the temple of the Holy Ghost which is in you, which ye have of God, and ye are not your own? For ye are bought with a price: therefore glorify God in your body, and in your spirit, which are God's."*
>
> *1 Corinthians 6:19-20*

Daniel Lowden
September 2011

OUR RESPONSIBILITY BEFORE GOD

The hypocrisy we must avoid:

> *"Woe unto you, scribes and Pharisees, hypocrites! for ye make clean the outside of the cup and of the platter, but within they are full of extortion and excess. Thou blind Pharisee, cleanse first that which is within the cup and platter, that the outside of them may be clean also."*
>
> *Matthew 23:25-26*

It has often been said: "The heart of the problem is the problem of the heart." This was certainly true of the Pharisees, and it is certainly true today. Whether we occupy ourselves with the latest worldly trends and fashions, or whether we perfect an outward display of religious respectability and correctness, many of us (and the writer is no exception) have fallen into the same sinful trap as the Pharisees. They were so preoccupied with the perfection of their external appearance, that they neglected the condition of their hearts. It was for this reason that the Lord Jesus called them 'blind'. They could not see the sin of their own hearts. They had concentrated so much time and effort on external perfection that they had blinded themselves, not only to the sinful condition of their hearts, but to the Lord Jesus Christ Himself, the very Messiah whose coming into the world was prophesied in the Scriptures.

The powerful condemnation of the Lord Jesus Christ upon the scribes and Pharisees in Matthew chapter 23 shows us the hypocrisy of these men. It serves as a serious lesson to believers today. We could be dressed immaculately, and have all the outward appearance of respectability, and yet still be corrupt in our hearts. In his epistle, James exhorted the believers: *"Draw nigh to God, and he will draw nigh to you. Cleanse your hands, ye sinners; and purify your hearts, ye double minded"* (James 4:8). James was addressing saved individuals who had believed in Jesus Christ, but they still had sin in their hearts that needed to be confessed and repented of.

To preach the Biblical standards of dress, therefore, without addressing the heart, is a fruitless exercise. We must ensure that our hearts are right before God in the first place. External correction and perfection are of no value in the sight of God, if the heart is not addressed.

> *"Search me, O God, and know my heart: try me, and know my thoughts: And see if there be any wicked way in me, and lead me in the way everlasting."*
>
> *Psalm 139:23-24*

> *"If we confess our sins, he is faithful and just to forgive us our sins, and to cleanse us from all unrighteousness."*
>
> *1 John 1:9*

If our hearts are fully yielded to the will of God, and we examine ourselves before Him in this manner of true confession and prayer, then following His standards for dress will be a matter of loving obedience to Him.

THE RESPONSIBILITY OF MEN

The responsibility the man must take:

"Ye have heard that it was said by them of old time, Thou shalt not commit adultery: But I say unto you, That whosoever looketh on a woman to lust after her hath committed adultery with her already in his heart."

Matthew 5:27-28

It is remarkable that the Lord Jesus Christ preached this solemn warning to men very early in His ministry. Indeed, we find it in the opening chapters of the New Testament, as part of the 'Sermon on the Mount' which begins in Matthew chapter 5. That indicates how much importance Christ placed upon this teaching. He placed the responsibility upon the *man, first.*

This is in accordance with God's order of creation, and points back to Genesis. In Genesis chapter 2, **God created the man first, and commanded the man first, before the woman was created,** not to eat of the tree of the knowledge of good and evil (Genesis 2:16-18). The responsibility was placed upon the man first, as the head of God's creation, to follow God's command, and to take the lead in this regard.

18

The man, therefore, **first,** is responsible for his eyes, and for how he looks at members of the opposite sex. The Lord Jesus was not teaching that men are not to look at women at all. That would be impossible. Rather, He was teaching men not to look at women *to lust after them.* He was dealing with the *motive.* He was dealing with *how* and *why* a man looked upon a woman. And if the motive was lust, then the evil act of adultery had already taken place in the man's heart, as far as God was concerned, even if the act itself never took place. This shows us how serious the matter of lust is, in the eyes of God. It is not to be treated lightly.

Consider the testimony of Job:

> *"I made a covenant with mine eyes; why then should I think upon a maid?"*
>
> *Job 31:1*

God said that Job was a man who *"feareth God, and esheweth evil"* (Job 1:8). He feared God, and shunned evil. Job, therefore, made this covenant with his eyes, to shun evil and not to think about another woman. However, we see in this verse the connection between the eyes, and the mind. Lust begins with the eyes, before thoughts and imaginations begin to form. And Job was innocent, because he had made this covenant with his eyes, first.

The example of Job speaks volumes to men today. How vital it is, that we follow this example daily. Most men, if they were honest, would have to admit that they have often failed to guard their eyes. Most men, including the writer, at some point, have allowed their eyes to wander where they should not. Because of this, some of us have been guilty of the very sin that Jesus condemned, in Matthew 5:27-28. The Lord Jesus was surely aware of this when He continued in Matthew 5:29:

> *"And if thy right eye offend thee, pluck it out, and cast it from thee: for it is profitable for thee that one of thy members should perish, and not that thy whole body should be cast into hell."*

The Lord Jesus did not compromise His preaching when He warned of the eternal penalty of sin. In the immediate context, in this case, the sin was the lust of the eyes. Thanks be unto the Lord Jesus Christ, that He Himself was to be our sin bearer. The child of God, therefore, who is truly born again, has had his sins washed away in the blood of Jesus Christ, *"the lamb of God which taketh away the sin of the world"* (John 1:29). Is the reader truly born again? If he or she is truly saved, then the penalty of sin has been paid. However, while we have the Spirit of God indwelling us, we still have our old sinful nature, the flesh. Consider Galatians 5:17:

> *"For the flesh lusteth against the Spirit, and the Spirit against the flesh: and these are contrary the one to the other: so that ye cannot do the things that ye would."*

There is a battle taking place between the old man and the new, between the flesh and the Holy Spirit. How is the battle to be won? We find the answer already given in the preceding verse, Galatians 5:16:

> *"This I say then, walk in the Spirit, and ye shall not fulfill the lust of the flesh."*

And again, in verse 18:

> *"But if ye be led of the Spirit, ye are not under the law."*

We see here that a daily walk with Christ, and obedience to the Spirit of God is the key to victory in this daily spiritual battle. If we are led by the Holy Spirit, the law cannot condemn us, because we will not give into the temptation of lustful thoughts which lead to the very works of the flesh that the law condemns. It is only when we give in to the lust of the flesh that we come under the law again because we resist the restraint of the Holy Spirit. Other passages, such as Ephesians chapter 6 for example, deal with this same constant spiritual warfare that the child of God will face. The key to victory is surrender and obedience to the Holy Spirit. And because all Scripture is given by inspiration of the Spirit of God, we must begin by obeying the Word of God.

> *"And if thy right eye offend thee, pluck it out, and cast it from thee..."*
>
> *Matthew 5:29*

In His teaching during the sermon on the mount, the Lord Jesus plainly commanded that whatever causes us to sin, whether it be an eye, or a hand, must be severely dealt with. We know that Christ did not literally mean that we should destroy members of our bodies. Rather, He was using a severe illustration to teach us how severely we must treat sin, and the cause of sin. The cause of the offence is to be utterly cast away. That is how drastic our measures are required to be in order to deal with sin. And it is no co-incidence that this teaching of our Lord followed immediately after His pronouncement on lust in the preceding verse.

> *"But I say unto you, That whosoever looketh on a woman to lust after her hath committed adultery with her already in his heart."*
>
> *Matthew 5:28*

The Lord would not give us a commandment and not enable us, by His Spirit, to fulfill it. Therefore, men have the ability, through Christ and the Spirit of God, to take absolute authority over their eyes, and refuse to allow them to look at anything which would cause them to lust.

Not only do men have the *ability* in Christ to take control of their eyes, but they have the *responsibility* also. And they have a responsibility to get rid of anything that would offend them, and cause them to sin. We must actively *turn our eyes away* from lust, from whatever source it comes from. If it is the television, turn it off, or dispose of it altogether. If it is the internet, do likewise. If it is a sport or hobby magazine, do likewise. If it is another item of entertainment, do likewise. If it is the manner of a woman's dress, likewise **we must obey the Lord's command, and refuse to look in a lustful manner.** If this means turning our eyes away, then, as difficult as this may prove to be, we have the peace of knowing that with His enablement, we are simply obeying the teaching of our Lord. As the hymn writer put it: *"Trust and obey, for there is no other way, to be happy in Jesus, but to trust and obey."*

The difficulty the man will face:

It is increasingly difficult for Christian men, in today's society, to guard their eyes. The television, advertising images in public spaces that verge on pornography, and the rampant immodesty of much of today's fashion clothing worn by young women, are among the chief causes of the difficulty facing Christian men today. One cannot walk through a street; one cannot enter a shop; one can hardly go anywhere in the world without noticing such things. Bold, tight fitting, sensual, provocative, revealing garments, designed by the fashion industry to expose or cling to the flesh and which draw inappropriate attention to the wearer, are commonplace. But what is even more disheartening is that one cannot even enter a 21st century evangelical church without being exposed to the same gross immodesty, because these styles are now commonplace among Christian women also. It is for this reason that we will be dealing specifically with the responsibility of Christian women later.

William P. Nicholson, the famous evangelist from County Down, was mightily used of God, and led thousands of people to saving faith in Christ through his gospel preaching during the early part of the 20th century. On one occasion, Mr. Nicholson preached a very strong message directed mainly to professing Christians. Consider the following extract from this sermon, preached in the Tent Hall, Glasgow, October 1929:

> *"In like manner also, that women adorn themselves in modest apparel, with shamefacedness and sobriety; not with broided hair, or gold, or pearls, or costly array; But (which becometh women professing godliness) with good works."*
>
> *1 Timothy 2:9*

"When you look today at the women in the streets, when you meet them, tell me, dear friends: Is there anything according to this pattern about their manner of dress? The very parts of your body that nature and modesty would dress with shamefacedness and modesty, according to the fashions are the very parts that are exaggerated, the very parts that are made conspicuous.....believe me, dear friends, it is a million times harder for a young fellow to keep his soul clean today than it was when I was a boy. It is tremendous the pace that Christian women are making today when it comes to a matter of their adornment."

What is astonishing is that this message was preached over eighty years ago. The above quotation is only a small extract. W. P. Nicholson quoted from numerous other texts of Scripture, and his sermon contains the strongest preaching that I have ever encountered on this subject. He had noticed a significant change in fashion. Not many years before, around the turn of the 20th century, modesty and decency, generally speaking, still prevailed. Long, loose fitting dresses and garments, which completely covered the body, were still worn by most women in the Edwardian era. However, within a relatively short space of time, standards had begun to slip. Hollywood, and the introduction of the movies, no doubt, had a profound influence. Styles of evening dresses etc., became more revealing and seductive, accentuating the female figure. The black and white movies of the 1920s and 1930s, such as those that featured Ginger Rogers and her dancing performances with Fred Astaire, undoubtedly popularized such styles. Slowly but surely, immodesty was becoming fashionable.

And W. P. Nicholson responded with his bold preaching. Truly this was a preacher who had *"no fellowship with the unfruitful works of darkness"* but rather reproved them. (Ephesians 5:11).

Consider how much worse the decline had become in the 1960s, when the 'mini-skirt' arrived on the scene. Mr. Nicholson did not live to see that era, but one might wonder how he would have responded in his preaching, had God spared him.

Mary Quant, a prominent fashion designer during the 1960s, is generally acknowledged to be the inventor of the mini-skirt. She is quoted as having wanted to design something for women that was 'daring' and 'controversial'. She certainly succeeded. Furthermore, Mary Quant succeeded in making the grossly indecent mini-skirt acceptable in everyday society. As a result, the moral climate of society, in recent times, has never been more corrupted than since that generation. Fashions may change, and the fashion industry may introduce new styles, or re-introduce old ones, but invariably, these are always designed to be sexually provocative. Truly we live in a *"crooked and perverse nation"* (Philippians 2:15). If Mr. Nicholson declared how difficult it was for a man to 'keep his soul clean' in the 1920s, it is immeasurably more difficult today.

However, in spite of the difficulty they face, Christian men still have the responsibility to obey the commandments of the Lord Jesus Christ as revealed in Scripture. We are responsible not to look at women to lust after them, regardless of how they are dressed. We must make that covenant with our eyes, as Job did (Job 31:1). As Christ commanded us to 'pluck out' the eye or 'cut off' the hand that offends us, and cast it from us, so must we take control of our eyes, and remove absolutely anything from our daily walk that would offend us and cause us to sin.

There is wise counsel in the following commandment found in Proverbs chapter 4:25-27:

> *"Let thine eyes look right on, and let thine eyelids look straight before thee. Ponder the path of thy feet, and let all thy ways be established. Turn not to the right hand nor to the left: remove thy foot from evil."*

The victory the man is promised and the purity he must seek:

> *"There hath no temptation taken you but such as is common to man: but God is faithful, who will not suffer you to be tempted above that ye are able; but will with the temptation also make a way to escape, that ye may be able to bear it."*
>
> *1 Corinthians 10:13*

This is a powerful promise that God gives us in His Word. God is faithful, and whatever temptation we face in this world, God has promised to enable us to overcome it. As men therefore, we have everything that we need, because God is faithful. And if He is faithful to us, then we must be faithful to Him, and walk in obedience to His commandments. Let us refuse to compromise our obedience to the Word of God.

Paul instructed Timothy to treat the younger women in his church *"as sisters, with all purity"* (1 Timothy 5:2). What a solemn charge this is. As men, we have a responsibility to obey the Word of God, as found in this command here given to the young man Timothy. We must treat our sisters in Christ with all purity. This begins with our eyes. Training our eyes never to wander is the best place to start. However, in spite of how much we train our eyes, we will still face difficulty. Immodest dress is as common now among Christians as it is in the world. It will be impossible not to notice certain immodest items of clothing at some point. This can be a terrible distraction to the Christian man who comes to his local church or assembly to serve, worship, participate in the Lord's Supper, and be taught from the Word of God or even to preach himself.

This neglect of modesty and propriety, sadly, is a violation of the clear teaching of 1 Timothy 2: 9-10. In Paul's first letter to Timothy, the *very first point* **of doctrine** he gives with regard to the women, is their manner of dress. God, in His infinite wisdom, would have known that the natural tendency of women in the church would lean towards *immodest* dress rather than modest dress. Furthermore, the natural tendency of men, in their old fallen nature, would be to notice this and become distracted by the temptation to look lustfully at their Christian sisters. Such a scenario would ruin the spiritual purpose for gathering together in the first place, namely, to exalt the name of Christ and to have all of their thoughts centred upon Him. Furthermore, their purity of fellowship as believers in Christ together would be ruined by fleshly, carnal thoughts and desires. It is no different for us today. And yet, if any vital doctrine has been neglected by the church, it is the doctrine of modesty. It is time for Christian men to take a stand for purity and holiness, and speak forth the teaching of the Word of God on the subject, that other Christian men and women may learn afresh the vital importance of these forgotten virtues.

The vanity the man must avoid:

"And the same John had his raiment of camel's hair, and a leathren girdle about his loins; and his meat was locusts and wild honey."

Matthew 3:4

In addition to the responsibilities of men toward the opposite sex, there are principles with regard to the man's own appearance that are clearly taught in Scripture.

It is no co-incidence that John the Baptist's clothing is mentioned and clearly described in the Word of God. The overriding principle we see from John's example, is that no aspect of his clothing contradicted his message. When John preached in the wilderness, there was no evidence of vanity in his character. His clothing may have been unusual and distinctive, but was not worldly or extravagant. It was similar to the clothing worn by the Old Testament prophet, Elijah. John's message was a message of repentance. His purpose was to point people to Christ, not to draw undue attention to himself in any way. His appearance, therefore, was fitting for the strong message that he preached.

There was nothing fashionable about John's manner of dress. We might say that he was the most unfashionable 'Baptist' preacher who ever lived. And yet, he was one of the most effective preachers who ever lived. Multitudes came to hear him preach in the wilderness. And as he pointed them to Christ, they came to him, confessing their sins, and were baptized.

Evidently, his appearance did not hinder the work of the Holy Spirit in bringing many souls to repentance.

There is a clear lesson here for men today. The unisex fashion movement, and the male grooming industry, with all their associated products, have done their utmost to influence men to become more vain about their appearance. This is achieved by the promotion of effeminate clothing, hairstyles, and even anti-aging products for men. If there is anything in the modern fashion industry today that would be guaranteed to ruin our testimony for Jesus Christ, it is effeminate styles and clothing for men.

Consider what God's Word declares in relation to this:

> *"Know ye not that the unrighteous shall not inherit the kingdom of God? Be not deceived: neither fornicators, nor idolaters, nor adulterers, NOR EFFEMINATE, nor abusers of themselves with mankind, nor thieves, nor covetous, nor drunkards, nor revilers, nor extortioners, shall inherit the kingdom of God."*

1 Corinthians 6:9-10

Notice, in the above passage, the clear connection between **"effeminate"** and **"abusers of themselves with mankind"**. It is a documented fact that most of the chief unisex fashion designers are homosexual men. It is also a known fact that their designs have influenced much of the clothing sold in mainstream unisex fashion stores. With their bold, loud, close-fitting styles, many items of male fashion clothing are designed to draw attention to the male physique, and to cause men to appear vain, ostentatious, muscular, or in some cases, effeminate. Indeed, just as the 'cut' of many female fashion clothing items are designed to be sexually provocative, so the 'cut' of many men's jeans, trousers, shirts, t-shirts etc., is designed to be 'sexy.' Recent styles and items such as 'low rise', 'low waist', 'boot cut', 'flared', 'skinny' jeans etc., often with fashionable rips or faded areas; 'sleeveless' or 'muscle top' t-shirts, 'fitted' or 'slim fit' shirts (often worn unbuttoned at the chest), tight fitting jackets with fashionable zips and stitching, etc., are designed to draw undue attention to the man, and to give him a 'cool', 'sexy' look. That is in accordance with the way of the world. But we are *not* to be conformed to the world.

Many Christian men, including the writer in the past, have been guilty of falling into the sinful trap of male pride and vanity, when purchasing some of the above items. To avoid this danger effectively, I have found that it is wise to avoid every single outlet that sells such clothing. If this involves choosing retail outlets that market their clothing to older buyers as opposed to the younger, then that is a small price to pay to honour the Lord with our manner of dress. If this means that young Christian men dress in a plainer fashion that is perhaps considered older than their years, this is a small sacrifice to make in order that we may *"adorn the doctrine of God our Saviour in all things"* (Titus 2:10).

Christian men who seek to please and obey their Master, Christ, in all things, should consider, and put into practice the following command:

"And why take ye thought for raiment? Consider the lilies of the field, how they grow; they toil not, neither do they spin: And yet I say unto you, That even Solomon in all his glory was not arrayed like one of these. Wherefore, if God so clothe the grass of the field, which today is, and tomorrow is cast into the oven, shall he not much more clothe you, O ye of little faith? Therefore take no thought, saying, 'What shall we eat?' or 'What shall we drink?'

or, 'Wherewithal shall we be clothed?' (For after all these things do the Gentiles seek:) for your heavenly Father knoweth that ye have need of all these things."

Matthew 6:28-32

Some have interpreted this passage to mean that God does not mind how we dress, since we are not to take any 'thought for raiment.' But that is not what Christ was teaching. He was teaching, rather, that we should not give this matter undue consideration or importance. By mentioning Solomon as an example, our Lord was referring to the 'glory' of clothing. He was preaching against the practice of giving so much time and attention to our clothing that we become unduly concerned about our appearance. He was teaching that no man in all his glory was as beautiful as the lilies of the field, and that if this was how God clothed the grass, how much more would He provide food, drink and raiment for us, and ensure that we are properly clothed? Christ's teaching here leaves no place for pride or vanity with regard to our appearance. Indeed, that was the way of the Gentiles, and it is the way of the world today.

This was also the way of the Scribes and Pharisees, who loved to wear 'long clothing', and who loved greetings in the marketplaces, and the uppermost rooms at synagogues, and the chief seats at feasts, etc. Because of their hypocrisy, the Lord Jesus condemned them openly in Matthew 23:1-39. He called them *"whited sepulchres",* who appeared outwardly beautiful, but within were full of *"dead men's bones and all uncleanness"* (Matthew 23:27). It is evident that, outwardly, these men were exceedingly vain, and inwardly, they were corrupt to the core. Their example surely serves as a warning to Christian men (and women) today not to follow their example. However, as it has often been said, *"the heart of the problem is the problem of the heart."* Their outward appearance was merely a reflection of the sinful condition of their hearts.

This teaches us that it is not sufficient alone for Christians to correct the outward appearance. The heart must first be addressed. This is not to suggest that we neglect our appearance entirely and allow ourselves to become 'unkempt'. If our hearts are right with God, the outward appearance ought to reflect this. Dignity, respectfulness, and modesty of appearance, together with a love for our neighbours by telling them of their need of salvation, should be evidence to the world that we belong to Jesus Christ, and not that we are vain, self-righteous hypocrites. We can be clean, neat, and tidy, without becoming vain. Some of us, of course, must also allow for circumstances connected with our occupations which require working clothes. Some of the disciples, after all, were fishermen. However, the Christian man (and woman) must not allow any worldly vanity to corrupt their daily walk with Christ. Consider the following exhortation from Paul to the young man Timothy:

> ***"Flee also youthful lusts, but follow righteousness, faith, charity, peace, with them that call on the Lord out of a pure heart."***

> *2 Timothy 2:22*

The authority the man must take:

"One that ruleth well his own house, having his children in subjection with all gravity; (For if a man know not how to rule his own house, how shall he take care of the church of God?)"

1 Timothy 3:4-5

If ever there were a time when this truth needed to be re-enforced from the pulpits, it is today. Men are commanded in Scripture not only to love their wives as Christ loved the church, but to rule and exercise authority in their homes. Christian women are commanded to submit to their husbands in all things as unto the Lord (see Ephesians 5:22-33). The wife and children therefore, out of obedience to God and His Word, are under the man's authority. This authority is God-given, and men are to rule and to lead both in the church (1 Timothy 2:11-15), and in the home, as clearly taught in the above passage.

Christian men have a responsibility, therefore, to ensure that their wives and daughters obey the Word of God with regard to 'modest apparel', since it is clearly commanded. In 1 Corinthians chapter 14, after Paul commands that women keep silence in the churches (1 Corinthians 14:34), he teaches: *"And if they will learn anything, let them ask their husbands at home..."* (1 Corinthians 14:35). Here, we see clearly that the man is the spiritual head and teacher in the home. And he is to teach his wife in spiritual matters, which of course encompasses the teaching of the Word of God. It is the man's responsibility to exercise that loving authority in the home as God's servant, and to instruct his wife and children in all these matters.

As an unmarried man at the time of writing, I cannot speak from experience. Some more mature Christian brethren, therefore, may consider it inappropriate for a younger man of limited preaching experience, to be instructing them as to how they ought to be leading their families. It is not the writer's intention to bypass the God-given authority of individual Christian men in their homes. I do, however, see these matters clearly in the Scriptures. And I have observed, to my dismay, that they have been severely neglected. Many wives and daughters of sincere Christian men are dressing in an extremely provocative manner. In many cases, during meetings, although they may have their heads covered in accordance with the teaching of 1 Corinthians chapter 11, the covering of the rest of their bodies is grossly inadequate. Or, if they are covered, they are covered in an extremely sensual manner with tight fitting clothing that accentuates the figure. Whilst the Christian women themselves are partly to blame, *the men* are responsible for teaching their wives and daughters. Their manner of dress, therefore, is a reflection of how well their husbands and fathers are carrying out their responsibilities.

In an age when feminism has been used by Satan to spread its subtle influence into every sphere of society, it is surely high time that Christian men took their responsibility seriously, and determined not to bow under the pressure of a society that is at enmity with the principles of God's Word. It is high time that men began to take authority in their homes, and in assemblies and churches.

In conclusion to this section, Christian men must take their God-given responsibilities seriously. We must exercise loving authority in our homes.

As previously outlined, we must flee the youthful lusts of vain, worldly fashion, and avoid dressing in a manner that contradicts our testimony for Christ. We must also flee the youthful lusts caused by immodest female fashion, and refuse to let our eyes look at anything that would cause us to lust. Let us follow Christ, and be *real* men.

"Watch ye, stand fast in the faith, quit you like men, be strong"

1 Corinthians 16:13

THE RESPONSIBILITY OF WOMEN

The modesty the woman must have:

> *"In like manner also, that women adorn themselves in modest apparel, with shamefacedness and sobriety; not with broided hair, or gold, or pearls, or costly array; But (which becometh women professing godliness) with good works."*
>
> *1 Timothy 2:9-10*

This is the first passage we come across in the New Testament which directly addresses the subject of women's clothing. As always with any study of the Scriptures, we must not ignore the context. In chapter 1, Paul had asked Timothy to remain in Ephesus and to *"charge some that they teach no other doctrine"* (1 Timothy 1:3). The apostle had left Timothy in charge of the church, that is, the 'saints and the faithful in Christ Jesus' (Ephesians 1:1), the body of believers at Ephesus. He then proceeded to instruct Timothy as to how meetings of believers were to be conducted. Throughout this epistle, and also 2 Timothy (as indeed in all the epistles), church truth, doctrine, and practice, are clearly outlined. Timothy was charged by Paul, before God, to *"preach the word; be instant in season, out of season; reprove, rebuke, exhort with all longsuffering and doctrine"* (2 Timothy 4:2). This teaching was not to be neglected. And in 1 Timothy chapter 2, the first activity that is mentioned is **prayer (v.1).** Prayer was to be the foundation of everything that was to follow; it was to be the the primary activity of the church. And *men* were to take the lead in this activity (see v. 8). This is a foundational principle of the New Testament, that *men*, not women, are to lead and exercise authority in the church.

Immediately following this passage giving clear instructions as to how and why men were to lead the ministry of prayer (v.1-8), we find this teaching on **"modest apparel"** in v.9. This shows us how serious and important a teaching modesty is. **It is not a 'secondary' doctrinal issue.** This is the very first reference to women that we find in this epistle. And in the context of the church gathering, the very first item that the apostle addresses concerning the women, **is their manner of dress.** Someone may ask, "why is this?" The first reason is very simple. It is one of the first aspects of a Christian gathering that people notice. Paul addresses this before moving on to the woman learning *"in silence with all subjection"* (v.11), and suffering her not to teach or to usurp authority over the man (v.12). Her place of subjection and silence in the church, therefore, is also to be reflected by her manner of dress.

But notice also, that Paul commands in v.9, *"In like manner also..."* This phrase refers back to the previous verse, commanding men to *"pray everywhere, lifting up holy hands, without wrath or doubting"* (v.8). This teaches us that **the manner of the men's prayers** is to be complimented by the **manner of the women's dress.** The modest manner of their dress should match the holiness of the men's prayers. **Both are of equal importance.** This, evidently, is a very high standard of modesty. Since this is God's standard of modesty, it must be completely different to the world's standards of dress.

A further reason why the manner of the women's dress was the very first point of doctrine given with regard to the role of women in the church, is implicit in the words *"modest apparel."* If there was a requirement for the Holy Spirit to stipulate this, we must conclude that, **1): It may not occur naturally to the women to dress in *modest* clothing.** 2): **The culture and society of that period in Ephesus and beyond, was not naturally inclined to be modest in behaviour, and this would have been reflected in some of the dress styles of the Gentile world.** The dress standards of society therefore, as is certainly the case today, would have inclined towards *sensuality* rather than *modesty.* There would have been a great temptation to the women, therefore, to conform to the world and yield to the lure of sensual attire. Such is certainly also the case today. Christian women are pressurized by the lure of the fashion retail stores, and all too often purchase those items of clothing which, by their nature, are designed to appeal to fleshly lusts.

We can conclude, therefore, that this teaching is given a place of prominent importance *for the moral protection of Christian men and women.* The apostle, under the divine direction of the Holy Spirit, taught women to dress in modest apparel, **as a matter of fundamental doctrine,** to protect men from the danger of lust, and from becoming distracted from their godly ministries and duties in the assembly; and to protect women from the danger of receiving lustful looks, and from their own natural inclination to follow the desires and fallen nature of the flesh by dressing in a sensual manner. It is no different today. All Scripture is given by inspiration of God (2 Timothy 3:16)

How modesty is defined in Scripture:

Paul continues in 1 Timothy 2:9, *"that women adorn themselves in modest apparel...".* What does the apostle mean by **'modest'**? Most of us, I believe, will have some understanding of what this word means in the Bible. It is the complete opposite of pride and sensuality. Consider the following words of the verse: *"with shamefacedness..."* This is a very strong word. Bible commentators, such as James Strong, have defined this word as meaning 'downcast eyes', godly 'bashfulness' (i.e, towards men), 'awe' (toward God); *(Strong's Exhaustive Concordance, Greek Dictionary Section, ref. no. 127).* The word itself shows us clearly that God intends for the woman to have an appropriate sense of shame. This is not a weakness. Rather, it is a strength worthy of great honour. It is where the expression *"have you no shame?"* comes from. It immediately causes us to think of female modesty and decency. It indicates a *shrinking away* from anything that is improper. 'Shamefacedness' is not a wrong attribute for a woman to have who fears God and loves Jesus Christ, and seeks to please Him in all things.

Since this includes the area of dress which is the first aspect addressed by Paul in this epistle, the godly, sincere woman of God will desire to please her Lord and Saviour by the manner in which she dresses. Her 'shamefacedness', therefore, should be entirely evident by her manner of dress. This, again, is an extremely high standard of modesty.

Paul continues in v.9, *"and sobriety...".* This word, of course, comes from the familiar word 'sober'. It means to have complete self-control, self-judgment, and restraint from anything that is inappropriate. Galatians 5:22-23 describes the fruit of the Holy Spirit: *"But the fruit of the Spirit is love, joy, peace, longsuffering, gentleness, goodness, faith, meekness, temperance: against such there is no law."* Note the word *'temperance'*. This means self-control. The God-fearing woman who is walking in the Holy Spirit (Galatians 5:25), will manifest this self-control in her daily walk with God. This must be reflected, therefore, by her manner of dress. The woman of God will restrain herself from wearing anything that draws undue attention to herself. She will restrain herself from any form of dress that is inappropriate or immodest.

These three simple terms in 1 Timothy 2:9, *'modest apparel'*, *'shamefacedness'*, and *'sobriety'*, show us clearly that God's standard for modest clothing is the very highest standard imaginable. We might say, in simple terms, that this is **what modesty *is*.**

The remainder of the verse, however, shows us **what modesty *is not:***

"...not with broided hair, or gold, or pearls, or costly array..." The apostle is not forbidding specific types of hair arrangement and jewellery. Rather, he is simply using examples of clothing and appearances which are extravagant, worldly, and ostentatious. Such clothing, hairstyles, or accessories, whatever the style or fashion, would draw undue attention to the woman because of their sensuality and worldliness. Such an outlandish appearance would be the very opposite of the previous description of modesty in the same verse. An Old Testament example of this is found in 2 Kings 9:30: *"And when Jehu was come to Jezreel, Jezebel heard of it, and she painted her face, and tired her head, and looked out at a window."*

We know that modesty was certainly not the reason why Jezebel 'painted her face.' We are also familiar with the sorry fate that met Jezebel shortly afterwards. In today's society, the cosmetics industry entices women to go to great expense in the excessive use of make-up and similar products. Indeed, brand names such as 'Max Factor', 'Loreal' etc., are promoted by successful, grossly indecent models and pop artists such as Kate Moss and Madonna. Such individuals have become role models for today's younger generation, encouraging women to reject all restraints of innocence and decency. Modern make-up products are sold to young women as accessories to gain a powerful and seductive influence over men in the realm of lust. Today they are even promoted to children. They merely add extra power to the seductive trap of immodest clothing styles. Modesty is certainly not on the agenda of the indecent models and pop stars who market such products.

However, in 1 Timothy 2:10, the Word of God describes how the woman of God is to be 'adorned': *"But (which becometh women professing godliness) with good works."* Note that this is directed to women who profess godliness. This applies to any woman who professes faith in Christ, and who has trusted Him for salvation, and is truly born again. **That which draws attention to the Christian woman who loves God, is her service to Him; her good works, not her fashion clothing or accessories.** Any bold, immodest, extravagant, provocative, sensual, worldly dress styles would contradict this profession of godliness.

These two very straightforward verses in Paul's first letter to Timothy, which directly address the subject of women's clothing, show us that God's standard of modesty is the complete opposite of the world's standard. It is the highest, holiest, most commendable standard imaginable. Indeed, it sets forth the standard so clearly that we could finish at 1 Timothy 2:9-10. But this is not the only place in Scripture where God's standards for clothing are outlined. The apostle Paul undoubtedly had all of these in mind when the Holy Spirit directed him to write the words 'modest apparel.' To ignore other relevant Scriptures, would not be consistent with what the apostle Paul declared in Acts 20:27: ***"For I have not shunned to declare unto you all the counsel of God."***

Fashions of clothing have changed throughout history and culture, but God has not changed. Malachi 3:6 declares: ***"For I am the Lord, I change not; therefore ye sons of Jacob are not consumed."*** Isaiah 40:8 declares: ***"The grass withereth, the flower fadeth: but the word of our God shall stand forever."*** It is clear, throughout Scripture, that God has not changed, and that His Word has not changed. Indeed, Psalm 119:89 declares: ***"Forever, O Lord, thy word is settled in heaven."*** If God and His Word have not changed, then the principles that we find in His Word, with regard to clothing, have not changed.

In the following sections we will examine some key passages of Scripture where God has clearly revealed His standards for clothing and dress.

How modesty was established from the very beginning:

> ***"And they were both naked, the man and his wife, and were not ashamed."***
>
> *Genesis 2:25*

In the beginning, when the man and the woman had been created by God, the serpent had not yet appeared, and had not yet deceived the woman. Man's fall, therefore, had not yet occurred; there was no knowledge of good and evil, and there was no sin. Therefore, there was no shame in their nakedness because they had not sinned, and had no awareness of sin. And since there was no sin attached to their nakedness, they did not need to be covered and so clothing had not yet come into existence. However:

> *"And when the woman saw that the tree was good for food, and that it was pleasant to the eyes, and a tree to be desired to make one wise, she took of the fruit thereof, and did eat, and gave also unto her husband with her; and he did eat. AND THE EYES OF THEM BOTH WERE OPENED, AND THEY KNEW THAT THEY WERE NAKED; and they sewed fig leaves together, and made themselves aprons."*
>
> *Genesis 3:6-7*

After the woman had been deceived by the serpent, and had fallen into sin by disobedience to God's command, along with her husband, the first consequence of their sin was that their eyes were opened, and they both became aware of their nakedness. Prior to this, they were both pure, and their eyes were pure. But now sin had entered into their hearts, and they were no longer pure. In contrast to the previous chapter when they were not ashamed of their nakedness, now they were ashamed because of their sin. Their first reaction, therefore, was an immediate attempt to cover themselves. But their attempt was without success. Consider what followed:

"And they heard the voice of the Lord God walking in the cool of the day: and Adam and his wife hid themselves from the presence of the LORD God amongst the trees of the garden."

Genesis 3:8

Even though they had made themselves fig-leaf aprons, they still hid themselves from the presence of the Lord as soon as they heard His voice. This shows us that they still feared the presence of the Lord, despite their attempt to cover themselves. This is obvious from Adam's response to God, because after God called unto Adam, **"Where art thou?"**, in v.9 (holding Adam accountable as the head of the woman), Adam replied:

"....I heard thy voice in the garden, and was afraid, BECAUSE I WAS NAKED, and I hid myself."

Genesis 3:10

What is remarkable about Adam's response to God, is that *he still considered himself to be naked,* in spite of his and his wife's attempt to cover themselves. **This shows us that Adam acknowledged his own standard of clothing to be insufficient to cover his nakedness, and therefore knew that it would not be acceptable to God.** We realise, of course, that this was not the only reason for Adam and his wife hiding themselves. The chief sin that they had both committed, was to disobey the commandment of the Lord not to eat of the tree of the knowledge of good and evil (Genesis 2:17). It was this sin that the Lord addressed directly, in v.11:

"And he said, Who told thee that thou wast naked? Hast thou eaten of the tree, whereof I commanded thee that thou shouldest not eat?"

Genesis 3:11

The first sin that Adam and his wife committed was to disobey the commandment of God and to eat of the tree that He had commanded Adam not to eat of. The first result of that sin was that their nakedness was now exposed to each of them, and that it needed to be covered. However, after the Lord had pronounced His judgments upon the serpent, the woman, and the man, notice what took place in v.21:

"Unto Adam also and to his wife did the Lord God make coats of skins, and clothed them." (Genesis 3:21)

This was the very first act that God carried out after His pronouncements of judgment. The fact that God made these 'coats' for Adam and his wife shows us clearly that their own attempts to clothe themselves were not acceptable to God. Notice the difference: In v.7, they *"...sewed fig leaves together, and made themselves APRONS."*

In v.21, God made them *"...COATS of skins, and clothed them."*

Their *aprons* only covered them **partially.** The *coats,* however that God provided for them covered them **completely.** The same Hebrew word for 'coats' is translated elsewhere in Scripture as **'robes'.** This refers to **a long, modest, loose-fitting garment.**

Here, we find a foundational principle of clothing in the Bible. As God required the man and the woman to be completely covered, **so God must also require our nakedness to be completely covered.** Indeed, consider Adam's reaction to God in the garden again. He said, *"I heard thy voice in the garden, and was afraid, because I was naked, and I hid myself"* (Genesis 3:10). He heard God's voice *after* he and his wife made fig-leaf coverings for themselves, and yet *he still referred to himself, in this state, as*

45

'naked.' He was acknowledging that the fig leaf coverings were grossly inadequate. And God did not disagree on that score. Therefore, **we must acknowledge that, in God's eyes, partial nakedness is still nakedness.** This principle was established by God immediately after the Fall, and we shall see that it is continued right throughout Scripture.

How modesty applies:

W e have seen from the commandment of the Lord Jesus to men in Matthew 5:28, that whoever looks at a woman to lust after her has committed adultery with her already in his heart. The Word of God consistently shows us that men, in their fallen sinful nature, are tempted *visually* by what they see. That is how David's sin with Bathsheba began, in 2 Samuel chapter 11, when he *saw* her from his roof. **However, in Leviticus 18:6-19, God clearly prohibits any uncovering of nakedness outside of marriage.** Bathsheba was equally guilty in the affair with David because she exposed herself by washing where a man could see her from his roof. **Since the fall of mankind, the public exposure of nakedness in the Bible is *always* associated with shame.** The woman of God, therefore, must ensure that she is fully, properly, and modestly covered.

THE BIBLE REFERS TO TWO SPECIFIC AREAS

1) The upper body, *specifically the area of the chest and bosom,* is referred to in Scripture, and is to be reserved only for marriage:

> *"Let thy fountain be blessed: and rejoice with the wife of thy youth. Let her be as the loving hind and pleasant roe; let her breasts satisfy thee at all times; and be thou ravished always with her love."*
>
> *Proverbs 5:18-19*

The union of the marriage bed is blessed of God if it is maintained in absolute sanctity. The uncovering of nakedness *within* marriage, and in absolute privacy, therefore, is right and pure. Hebrews 13:4 tells us:

> *"Marriage is honourable in all, and the bed undefiled: but whoremongers and adulterers God will judge."*

When nakedness is uncovered *outside* marriage, this is wrong and impure, and is condemned by God, and will not go unpunished.

For a Christian woman even to partially expose, or wear clothing that draws attention to the bosom which is reserved only for marriage, and which only her husband should see, **is a violation of the sanctity of marriage.** This applies also to the unmarried woman, since her future husband (if she marries), should only see this. Here we find a foundational principle, that *the upper area of the woman's body is to be fully and modestly covered.*

We can reasonably accept from God's Word that the upper body includes every area of the chest, waist, and back.

There are many styles of upper garments and one-piece dresses which deliberately reveal a large portion of the upper chest and breast area, and are made even more revealing by bending or moving a certain way. These most certainly could not be described as modest. However, exposing even small areas of skin in certain places can be an enormous distraction, and can cause men to be tempted in the visual realm of lust. The reason for this, is that it creates the enticing effect of a 'sample' of that which is forbidden. The fashion industry expertly understands this sensual effect, and designs its' products accordingly. There are certain 'racy' styles of dresses and 'tops' for example, which may cover the chest area, but which have provocative, suggestive 'slits' or 'cut-outs' in the front or back, exposing just enough flesh to draw a man's attention and to cause him to look in a lustful manner. Many of these 'slits' or 'cut-outs' are subtle in their design, and are usually placed in an area where an undergarment can be seen. However, some styles of upper garments go even further with this design to provoke male lust. There are some styles of blouses, for example, that are literally transparent or 'see-through' in their design, sometimes referred to as 'sheer' blouses. Often these are worn with only an undergarment underneath. Even if a man *instantly* turns his eyes away, the damage of a split second 'glimpse' is enough to defile the mind because of the instant disturbing effect of visual lust.

Furthermore, the gross immodesty of 'backless' evening gowns, or figure-hugging evening dresses which completely expose the shoulders, cannot be underestimated. Also, very slim fitting t-shirts and sleeveless tops, or 'tank tops' which accentuate the breast area or expose the stomach and waist area, t-shirts with suggestive 'slashes', tops with very low hem lines down the middle chest area, and many other similar items, are designed to expose flesh and entice inappropriate looks. The Christian woman ***"professing*** *godliness"* (1 Timothy 2:10) ought to understand that there is no excuse for a woman of God to be wearing any such sensual and indecent clothing.

By mentioning these items, I may be accused by some of 'legalism', or 'splitting hairs'. But consider 1 Timothy 2, v.9 again, and ask the simple question: could any of these styles of dress be described as **'modest'**? Consider Genesis chapter 3 again. God **did not accept** the fig-leaf aprons that the man and the woman made for themselves. This shows us that God did not accept a **'partial'** covering; *their standard of dress was not acceptable to God.* When God clothed them with 'coats of skins' (Genesis 3:21), God's standard was to cover their nakedness completely, and modestly. Also, *God made these garments Himself.* That shows us that we do not have the liberty to set our own standards of modesty, or decide for ourselves what is acceptable or unacceptable. God established the standards at the beginning, and God has not changed. He most certainly would not have allowed any low hem lines, slits or cut-outs in those garments. God ensured that those garments left **no area of flesh indecently exposed.** If we are to follow God's standard of modesty, then this is foundational. The woman's upper body is her own and her husband's, and must be fully and modestly covered. Secondly:

2) The lower body, *specifically the legs and thighs,* are referred to in Scripture:

> *"Come down, and sit in the dust, O virgin daughter of Babylon, sit on the ground: there is no throne, O daughter of the Chaldeans: for thou shalt no more be called tender and delicate. Take the millstones, and grind meal: uncover thy locks, make bare the leg, uncover the thigh, pass over the rivers. Thy*

> **nakedness shall be uncovered, yea, thy shame shall be seen: I will**
> **take vengeance, and I will not meet thee as a man."**
>
> *Isaiah 47:1-3*

This passage describes God's judgment upon Babylon, who is portrayed here as a woman. The judgment begins by declaring that she would no longer be called 'tender' and 'delicate', but would carry out laborious tasks such as grinding meal, suggesting humiliation. Then, in addition to this, she is commanded to uncover her hair, followed by the leg, and then the thigh. By doing this, God declared that her nakedness would be uncovered, and her shame would be seen. We can conclude therefore, that exposure of flesh **in public** is something to be ashamed of, not something to flaunt or to be proud of.

Notice also, in this passage, that there is a distinction between the lower and upper legs. Quite simply, the more of the leg that is revealed, the more shameful the nakedness becomes. It is no co-incidence that the expression *'below the knee'* is often applied by Christians who have firm convictions on the subject of female modesty and standards for the length of skirts and dresses. Even in secular society, there are compulsory standards for the length of skirts in uniforms worn by women employed by professional institutions such as banks, airlines and travel agencies, for example. We would acknowledge without question that the thighs, specifically, are the woman's nakedness and that the Christian woman should never wear clothing which reveals or accentuates these. However, this is not a license to expose or draw inappropriate attention to the lower legs. There are many provocative styles of shoes and boots with high heels, for example, which accentuate the lower legs in a sensual manner, and we will address these more specifically in the next section. Often, in Christian circles, these are worn with skirts or dresses that only just reach the knee in length, and a mere 'flash' of the leg can be just as provocative. I have read numerous testimonies from men who responded to the survey contained in David W. Cloud's book *Dressing for the Lord* which bear witness to that very fact. I am convinced, therefore, and would urge Christian women, that the legs should be *entirely covered.*

Thus, we can see from these Scriptural references to both the lower and upper body that the Bible makes clear what it is to expose nakedness. Any item which enhances, exposes, or draws attention to the legs or chest could not be described as modest.

Short skirts and dresses, which expose and draw attention to the thighs, are most certainly not modest. As mentioned earlier in the men's chapter, Mary Quant was the fashion designer of the 1960s who is generally acknowledged to be the inventor of the 'mini-skirt'. She admitted that her intention was to 'entice men', and to be 'daring' and 'controversial'. Some European countries banned the mini-skirt when it was introduced in the mid-1960s, because they believed that it would lead to incidents of rape. However, Quant succeeded in making the grossly indecent mini-skirt generally acceptable in society, and our culture has never been the same since. Fashions may change, and items like the mini-skirt may come in and out of fashion, but, we must remember, that whether or not an item such as a mini-skirt is fashionable is not the determining factor when making a decision as to whether or not to wear it. The determining factor for the Christian woman is what God has commanded, and what the Bible states with regard to what is modest.

At the time of writing, very short skirts, and dresses, which expose a large proportion of the upper legs, are extremely common among young women, and young Christian women are no exception. Some of these are so short that they are virtually identical to the mini-skirt of the 1960s. These seem to be frequently worn with tights or 'leggings', as if that somehow rendered them more decent. Nothing could be further from the truth. The legs may be 'covered', but not *modestly* covered. All that items such as tights and leggings do, is to enhance and outline the shape of the area of body they are supposed to cover. In most cases they draw just as much attention as if the legs were not covered in the first place. Equally immodest is the common trend of wearing very tight 'leggings' with only a t-shirt or upper garment over them which is grossly insufficient in length, or in some cases nothing over them at all, drawing attention to those areas of the body which are completely forbidden outside of marriage. We must not underestimate also, the sinfulness of some 'evening' dresses. In addition to those which expose the back or chest, there are some which are 'slashed' at the legs in a highly provocative manner, from long at one side to short at the other, or from long at the rear to short at the front, etc. A formal occasion is no excuse for a Christian to dress in such a manner. Such clothing could certainly not be described as 'modest apparel'.

In the summer season, particularly during warm sunny weather, the boundaries of immodesty are pushed to even further extremities. The same 'mini-skirt' styles of short skirts and dresses mentioned above, are worn by young women on the streets with the legs completely uncovered. Or, in other cases, young women appear in public wearing indecent, tight fitting shorts, or 'cut-off' denim shorts, sometimes referred to as 'hot-pants'. Most older generations of Bible- believing Christians would agree that most female shorts, regardless of their style, for obvious reasons, are immodest. But the current styles that are worn on the streets in the summer season are so 'skimpy' that even a mere accidental split-second glimpse causing a man to notice, is enough to defile his mind and lead to lustful thoughts. As mentioned earlier, this is part of the daily spiritual battle that the Christian man faces. It is the Christian woman's responsibility to do her utmost not to cause her brother to stumble, as much as it is the man's responsibility to obey Christ and not to allow his eyes or his mind to wander into lust.

Earlier this year, I heard a radio interview with a number of young women on a city-centre street in Belfast. The radio journalist asked for their comments on the spell of warm weather and sunshine that they were experiencing at that time. They all responded with great enthusiasm, **and the one benefit they all mentioned without exception, was the opportunity to *wear less clothing.*** I was dismayed, but not surprised. It seems that many young women find sunny weather to be the perfect excuse to expose themselves in even more bold and daring ways, and to draw as much attention to their bodies as possible, in full view of the public eye. As we examine further the subject of immodest dress styles in the light of Scripture in the following sections, we shall see that nothing even remotely resembling the previously mentioned styles are fitting for a Christian woman who professes godliness.

The immodesty the woman must avoid:

> *"Moreover the LORD saith, Because the daughters of Zion are haughty, and walk with stretched forth necks and wanton eyes, walking and mincing as they go, and making a tinkling with their feet: Therefore the Lord will smite with a scab the crown of the head of the daughters of Zion, and the LORD will discover their secret parts. In that day the Lord will take away the bravery of their tinkling ornaments about their feet, and their cauls, and their round tires like the moon, the chains, and the bracelets, and the mufflers, the bonnets, and the ornaments of the legs, and the headbands, and the tablets, and the earrings, the rings, and nose jewels, the changeable suits of apparel, and the mantles, and the wimples, and the crisping pins, the glasses, and the fine linen, and the hoods, and the vails. And it shall come to pass, that instead of sweet smell there shall be stink; instead of a girdle a rent; and instead of well set hair baldness; and instead of a stomacher a girdling of sackcloth; and burning instead of beauty."*

> *Isaiah 3:16-24*

The above passage certainly does not make pleasant reading. Nevertheless we must accept that it is the Word of God, and it shows us that God utterly detested the immodest dress styles of the daughters of Zion, who were His own people. As we have already established, God has not changed, and therefore His judgment concerning immodest clothing has not changed. If his judgment was about to fall upon the women of Israel at that time because of their immodesty, then God is certainly not pleased with the immodest dress standards of women today, nor with any Christian who dresses in a similar manner.

However, notice first of all that God addressed *their hearts:*

> *"Moreover the LORD saith, because the daughters of Zion are haughty..."*
>
> Isaiah 3:16

God was able to see right into the hearts of the daughters of Zion. He was able to see the motives that lay behind their immodest dress. They were **'haughty'.** They were proud, rebellious and arrogant; the very opposite of the character of the godly woman we have already seen described in the New Testament, who is a woman of *'shamefacedness'*, *'sobriety'*, *and* *'good works'* **(1 Timothy 2:9-10).** Paul also describes to another church overseer, Titus, what should characterise the godly woman. She is to be *'discreet'* and *'chaste'* **(Titus 2:5).**

These attributes of godly women are the very opposite of the manner and behaviour of the daughters of Zion, who were *'haughty'.* Instead of *'shamefacedness'*, they had no shame, and were conducting themselves in a proud and ungodly manner. Instead of *'sobriety'*, they had no restraint, and this manifested itself in their haughtiness and manner of dress. Instead of *'good works'*, they evidently devoted much of their time to fashion, and displaying their items of fashion in public. Isaiah 3:16-24 is reminiscent of a high-profile fashion show, or a Hollywood film awards ceremony. Instead of being *'discreet'*, they had no discretion whatsoever, but paraded themselves openly in a manner that drew undue attention to themselves. And instead of being *'chaste'*, they were carnal and sensual, and they undoubtedly caused men to lust after them because of their behaviour and their immodest clothing. **Fundamentally,** the problem lay in the hearts of these women, because they were haughty. This proves that their hearts were in rebellion against God, and this rebellion manifested itself in their manner of dress.

FEMINISM AND FASHION

It is remarkable that this very same attitude of 'haughtiness' exists today. The evil influence of feminism goes hand in hand with the immodest fashion culture, encouraging women to reject the natural characteristics of feminine modesty that God created them to have. Consider how Peter describes this modesty:

> *"Likewise, ye husbands, dwell with them according to knowledge, giving honour unto the wife, as unto the weaker vessel, and as being heirs together of the grace of life; that your prayers be not hindered."*
>
> *1 Peter 3:7*

Peter, under Divine inspiration, describes the woman of God as the *'weaker vessel'*. This does not in any way suggest inferiority. Rather, it is in accordance with God's order of creation. In Genesis chapter 2, the woman was created as the 'help-meet' for the man. She was given to the man to help him, and to be protected by him. We can see how the daughters of Zion in Isaiah chapter 3 rejected this godly characteristic of their femininity. Just a few verses before the above passage in 1 Peter chapter 3, the apostle instructs women to be in subjection to their own husbands, and then describes what the heart of true modesty is, which we will examine in closer detail later. These characteristics of submission, subjection and modesty are the very opposite of what is promoted by today's popular culture. Instead of the 'weaker vessel', women today are encouraged to believe that they are the stronger and superior sex. They are likewise encouraged by the fashion industry to dress in a bold, brash, domineering, and sexually provocative manner. They are encouraged by society and the media to be independent, powerful, and successful; to 'rise to the top' by gaining promotion, or by gaining managerial or executive positions in their employment and professions, or by running their own enterprises, or by achieving fame in pop music.

A few years ago I heard a brief radio interview with a woman on the subject of equal opportunities in the workplace. In her own exact words, "managing men", and "how we should manage men in the workplace" were among the expressions that she used to explain her views. Such expressions are an accurate description of current trends which reflect the modern feminist agenda. Women are encouraged to gain controlling influence over men in the realms of careers, politics, business, and even marriage and relationships (this is not to ignore the problem of domestic abuse, however the increasing influence of feminism is certainly a contributing factor to the causes of such abuse, whether it is the male or female partner who is the perpetrator).

The media often features women campaigning aggressively against 'gender discrimination'. Often, they are dissatisfied that there is still a male majority in many professional fields, and want to see more women in positions of power in every area of society. Recently, I even heard a brief article on Radio Ulster, of a survey suggesting that an increasing number of 'high-flying' professional women will require their spouses to become 'house husbands' in order to help their female partners to successfully pursue their careers. The female journalist who gave the report then jokingly ordered her husband at home to fill the dishwasher. Such an attitude is typical of the contemporary feminist philosophy. They have despised and rejected the Biblical role for the woman that God has clearly revealed in His Word. This modern form of feminism is subtle, but very aggressive. It is reflected by modern female fashion which is imposing, domineering, and provocative. The Christian woman should be discerning, and recognise the subtle but powerful influence of feminism in every sphere of society, and utterly reject it.

PROMINENT MODERN-DAY EXAMPLES OF IMMODESTY

Isaiah 3:16-24 is a remarkably accurate description of the modern fashion culture that prevails today. After first addressing the problem of their hearts, God, through His prophet Isaiah describes the manner in which they carried themselves when they walked:

> *"...and walk with stretched forth necks and wanton eyes, walking and mincing as they go, and making a tinkling with their feet:"*

Isaiah 3:16

Their posture, as they walked, with their necks stretched forth, indicates a proud, provocative, imposing manner. It also indicates a 'demanding' attitude; evidently they were demanding male attention wherever they walked. This is also shown by their *'wanton eyes'*. Their eyes were continuously looking around for attention, and 'wanton' suggests that they were never satisfied. The more attention they received, the more they wanted. They evidently wanted men to look at them lustfully, in exactly the manner that Christ preached against in Matthew chapter 5.

'Mincing' means to walk in a seductive, provocative manner. And as they walked along, they made a noise with their feet. Whatever they wore on their feet, made a 'tinkling' noise while they walked in this provocative manner. This description is strikingly familiar when we consider what the fashion industry produces today to cause a similar effect. Items of footwear with very high heels, for example, 'stiletto' heels, are designed to make a loud 'tapping' noise and to draw attention to the woman as she walks. These often give the woman an ostentatious and imposing look, elevate her figure in a sensual manner, and cause her to walk in this very same 'mincing' manner as the daughters of Zion. It is exactly the same manner that is seen on the 'cat-walks' of wicked fashion shows and in profane Hollywood movies.

I remember, many years ago, as a child, viewing part of a television programme with my parents, on the history of 'stiletto' heels. I remember two specific details that were mentioned. Firstly, early examples of footwear with high 'stiletto' heels were modelled by Hollywood movie actresses. Secondly, one word was used to describe them: **'naughty'**. In fact, the programme emphasised that they were *purposely designed* to be 'naughty'. Even as a child, I knew what that suggested. Stiletto heels pushed the boundaries of decency, and by their nature were suggestive of 'naughty' behaviour. What does the Bible say in response to this? Consider the reproof of James:

> *"Wherefore lay apart all filthiness and superfluity of NAUGHTINESS, and receive with meekness the engrafted word, which is able to save your souls."*
>
> *James 1:21*

'**Naughtiness**' is suggestive of many things. It indicates a kind of behaviour which is flirtatious, mischievous, sensual, and provocative. If such items of fashion accessories as high-heeled footwear were originally designed with these characteristics, and were suggestive of 'naughtiness', they could not possibly be consistent with the 'shamefacedness' and 'sobriety' of a sincere Christian woman. On the basis of the purpose for which they were designed, high heels could not be described as modest. Even if the Christian woman herself never behaves in a 'naughty' manner, and yet wears such fashion accessories that suggest the opposite of chastity and modesty, the inconsistency of such a testimony for Christ cannot be overlooked. Such characteristics of immodesty should be completely shunned by the woman who loves Christ and seeks to please Him with her modesty.

What is remarkable, as we read Isaiah chapter 3, is that every single item of apparel worn by these women is specifically mentioned. Here, we have an 'itemised' list of every single piece of clothing that God was displeased with. Consider this example:

> *"In that day the Lord will take away the bravery of their tinkling ornaments about their feet..."*
>
> *Isaiah 3:18*

The word '**bravery**' indicates that very same attitude that we find in the modern fashion culture today; a smug, arrogant, proud, self-assured confidence. Again, we find the 'tinkling ornaments' mentioned; these must have been the same items on their feet that made the 'tinkling' noise described in v.16, similar to the provocative high heels of today, and we see that these are associated with this '**bravery**'; a bold, brazen, haughty attitude. This is the very opposite of '**modest**'. It is also the opposite of 'shamefacedness' and 'sobriety' that we read of in 1 Timothy 2:9. It is the complete opposite of true Biblical modesty.

Consider another example: *"the ornaments of the legs..."* (v.20)

Their legs may have been at least partly covered, but were not covered modestly. Whatever these ornaments were, they drew inappropriate attention to the legs. At the time of writing, ladies' leather boots with high heels that reach to the knee in height (or even higher in some cases), are very popular, particularly in the winter season. They are a common sight in evangelical churches and assemblies. These became very prominent in the 1960s and 1970s together with the mini-skirt, and have come in and out of fashion regularly ever since, in various styles. Now they are so common that most women of various ages own a pair of them. Often they are worn with a skirt or dress which is above the knee in length, or over the top of tight-fitting trousers or leggings, making them all the more noticeable. Because of their design, most styles of ladies' boots accentuate the lower legs in a provocative manner, elevate the woman's stature in a sensual and imposing fashion, and often invite a man's eyes to look upwards and downwards in a lustful manner. There may be some styles with flat soles which are more ordinary in their design, and if covered by a long dress or skirt may be perfectly modest and practical for warmth and comfort in the winter. However, many styles of ladies' boots (including 'cowboy' styles which do not have high heels but which still make a loud 'tapping' noise when the individual walks) are *purposely designed* to be sensual and provocative, *and from a man's perspective, it is impossible not to notice them, due to their provocative styling.* Consider the word *'bravery'* in Isaiah chapter 3. Boots are often associated with power and authority. This was demonstrated, for example, by the German Nazi uniforms during World War Two. Provocative ladies' boots are designed to give women a sense of 'bravery';

i.e., power and influence over men. Such 'ornaments of the legs', could not be described as modest, and do not reflect a meek and quiet spirit of humble submission in the Christian woman.

Some may consider my mentioning such items to be 'trivial'. Again, I may be accused of 'legalism'. I believe, however, that when God inspired Paul to teach and command women to *"adorn themselves in modest apparel"* (1 Timothy 2:9), He would not have accepted **partial modesty.** Indeed, many Christian women have enough discernment to wear dresses and skirts that are modest in length and style, but the purpose of modesty is often defeated by wearing items such as provocative knee-high leather boots or shoes with very high heels. *The combination of a modest dress and sensual footwear is inconsistent.* Even worse, is to wear a skirt that is very short or tight fitting, with high-heeled shoes or boots. Such an outfit would generally only have been associated with prostitution in the past. Yet now, short or tight-fitting skirts and high-heeled footwear are commonly worn by Christian women. Also, some skirts and dresses, regardless of their length, are immodest by nature because of the material they are made from. Skirts made of leather or very shiny material for example, are, by their nature, designed to be sensual and suggestive. Again, the body may be covered, but not modestly.

These are only a few examples from the long list of clothing items that are specifically mentioned in Isaiah chapter 3. Provocative 'leggings' worn uncovered, tights with loud patterns or transparent designs, figure-hugging leather trousers, and other similar items, are just a few more examples of 'ornaments of the legs' which I have witnessed being adorned by women at various evangelical Christian gatherings. All the other items mentioned in Isaiah chapter 3, were clearly designed for the sole purpose of drawing attention to the women of Zion in a sensual fashion. They show us that although the daughters of Zion may have been 'clothed', they were certainly not clothed modestly. Because of their immodesty, the Lord's judgment upon them was extremely severe. I do not wish to intimidate or to offend Christian women by quoting this passage. But I earnestly entreat them to 'search the Scriptures' themselves, consult with their husbands and fathers, and seek God's guidance from His Word, to be led by the Holy Spirit, and not the flesh, with regard to choosing clothing that is modest.

FURTHER EXAMPLES:
TIGHT FITTING AND REVEALING CLOTHING

Just as the women of Israel in Isaiah chapter 3 were not dressed modestly, and perhaps only 'partially' covered; I must re-emphasise the extremely immodest effect of **tight fitting** clothing. I make a point of this because this phenomenon is so common and widespread not only in society, but among professing Christians today. The fashion industry understands the effect of tight fitting garments extremely well, and designs such products with the sole purpose of appealing to the fleshly lusts of both the wearer and the observer. Tight clothing is made from a variety of materials including leather, PVC, nylon, lycra, spandex, cotton or denim mixed with synthetic fibres, and various other substances. Such garments are purposely made to enhance and outline the shape of the body in a sensual fashion. Items such as uncovered leggings and tights, jeans, trousers, skirts, shorts, dresses, shirts, tops and blouses that cling to the female figure, enhance and draw attention to those areas of the body that only her husband should see, and should **never** be exposed. Again, God clearly forbids the uncovering of nakedness outside of the marriage bed, and we have already referred to those passages of Scripture that prove this. Tight clothing draws attention to that nakedness, i.e., the chest, thighs, posterior, and other parts of the body,

without the need to uncover them. Such clothing should be completely shunned by Christian women professing godliness.

I also urge women, again, to recognise the extremely immodest effect of wearing clothing that is **slightly or moderately revealing.** 'Slits' or 'cut-outs' in the upper area of dresses, as mentioned earlier, either in the back or front, are designed to expose **a small area of skin in an extremely suggestive manner.** We may also mention the immodest effect of low 'V' shaped necklines, low-cut tops, blouses and tops with mere straps in the upper area of the shoulder, 'evening' and 'formal' dresses that reveal a large portion of the chest or back, etc. On past occasions, I have even been shocked by some wedding dresses that have some or all of the above features.

Furthermore, many skirts and dresses, of various lengths, feature provocative 'slits' that reveal a portion of the leg or thigh when the woman walks. Some may argue that these are for practical purposes, to provide ease of movement when walking. But I would emphasise, in response to this, that if the long dress or skirt were sufficiently loose fitting in the first instance, this would not be necessary. Indeed, some 'long' skirts and dresses are so tight fitting that they defeat the purpose of modesty in the first place. Even worse, are tight fitting skirts and dresses that are above the knee or even shorter in length, and feature these same suggestive 'slits' in various places.

Low-cut, tight fitting jeans and trousers, also, are frequently worn with 'short cropped' tops, t-shirts, sweatshirts, etc. These garments often only just meet in the middle waist area, or in some cases do not meet at all. There is no other way to mention this, but when the woman wearing these bends or moves in a certain way, the gross immodesty which occurs when the area around the hips, waist, and posterior is exposed, cannot be underestimated.

It is destructive and defiling to the purity of mind for any Christian man who happens to be nearby and notices such indecency, even momentarily, through no fault of his own. Furthermore, (and I would prefer not to mention this since it is extremely embarrassing, nevertheless it has been a common occurrence among young Christian women and therefore needs to be reproved), even profane styles of undergarment have been revealed by this action. Such popular items are evil inventions of the fashion industry and by their nature are utterly wicked and shameful.

Some may respond: **"It is your fault for noticing."** However, the fact remains that in most cases, *it is impossible not to notice these things, even if a man instantly looks away. And even if the man is not looking in that direction, such gross immodesty cannot even fail to be noticed OUT OF THE CORNER OF A MAN'S EYE, EVEN WHEN HE IS NOT LOOKING IN THE WOMAN'S DIRECTION.* Low cut blouses, t-shirts, and tops, that reveal an area of the upper chest and bosom, create a similar effect of extreme immodesty when the women bends or moves in a certain manner. The Christian woman, who loves Christ, and professes godliness, should know and obey the Scriptures, and utterly reject all such styles.

GOD-ORDAINED DISTINCTIONS VIOLATED BY UNISEX FASHION CLOTHING

Consider the following Scripture:

"The woman shall not wear that which pertaineth unto a man, neither shall a man put on a woman's garment: for all that do so are an abomination unto the LORD thy God."

Deuteronomy 22:5

65

Although most Christian readers would agree that the worst form of violation of this commandment would be 'transvestite' or 'transgender' cross-dressing, the unisex fashion movement has sought to destroy the God-ordained distinctions between male and female. Some argue that to quote from the above verse to teach this principle is a misuse of Scripture. After all, just a few verses later, God commanded the children of Israel not to sow their vineyards with 'divers seeds' (Deuteronomy 22:9), and not to wear a garment of 'divers sorts' such as wool and linen together (v.11). Furthermore, He also commanded 'fringes' to be upon the four quarters of a person's vesture (v.12). However, in relation to clothing, consider which of these verses in Deuteronomy chapter 22 is given the greatest emphasis. Verse 5, in which men and women are commanded not to wear one another's clothing, is the only verse which contains the solemn warning:

"...for all that do so are an abomination unto the LORD thy God."

This is no co-incidence. Whilst the other commandments with regard to clothing that followed this verse were equally important, and specifically related to Israel, the principle of distinction between the sexes in verse 5 is given the greatest emphasis. It is also clearly repeated, with respect to natural appearance, in the New Testament:

"Doth not even nature itself teach you, that if a man have long hair, it is a shame unto him? But if a woman have long hair, it is a glory to her: for her hair is given her for a covering. But if any man seem to be contentious, we have no such custom, neither the churches of God."

1 Corinthians 11:14-16

Clothing is not mentioned in these verses, but if the principle of clear distinction between the male and female appearances is re-emphasised in the

New Testament, it naturally follows that this principle should apply when we consider what is **'modest apparel'.**

Perhaps the most common example of unisex clothing today is the trouser. Ironically, some ladies' trousers (particularly those designed for older women) are more modest than some skirts because of their loose-fitting design. However, in its' efforts to target younger buyers, the fashion industry has taken the trouser and has transformed it for younger women to deliberately accentuate those areas of the body that should never be revealed outside marriage.

Tight fitting trouser-suits, and figure-hugging trousers or jeans, in various styles such as 'skinny', 'flared', 'hipster', etc., often designed to sit very low at the waist, and tight around the thighs and posterior, destroy every trace of feminine modesty and decency.

The decline of modesty:

In contrast to all of the immodest clothing styles previously outlined, why were the dresses and clothing items of the Victorian era (1800s) designed the way they were designed? The answer is because society at that time in general, had a higher regard for Biblical principles and morality. Although drunkenness, adultery, crime and other corrupting influences were prevalent in society then just as they are today, they were not as obvious as today. Generally speaking, there was still a high public regard for modesty and decency. It is for this reason that the dresses designed for women in the Victorian era, and in the Edwardian era that followed, were very elegant, wide and loose fitting, and reached almost to the ground in length. Their upper garments also, were very modest, covering their entire upper bodies right up to the neck. The overriding impression of such clothing was this: **the entire body, from the neck down to the foot, was completely covered. Not only were the women fully covered, but NO part of their bodies was enhanced by any immodest, tight fitting or revealing clothing.**

It was also customary practice, in those times, for women who wore modest skirts and dresses to ride horses in the 'side-saddle' position for obvious reasons relating to modesty. Furthermore, I understand that during Victorian times, even the wooden legs of some furniture items were covered because their carved design resembled the shape of female legs. This may seem obsessive in the extreme to us today, but it shows us the extent of such caution to prevent lustful imaginations.

However, it was not long before standards began to slip, but **only slightly.** And this, I believe is the key to understanding how, within less than a century, modesty and decency were completely overturned, and replaced by immodesty and indecency. The change that occurred **was gradual but progressive.** I understand, that following the death of Queen Victoria in 1901, women began to wear skirts and dresses that were several inches from the ground in length, showing their feet. Previously, they were longer than this and covered the feet completely. There was a strong public reaction to this from some quarters, claiming that standards of decency were falling. This may seem ridiculous to many of us today. Indeed, the books of photographs from the late 1800s and early 1900s which I have in my possession show that by today's standards, the level of female modesty at that time was very high indeed.

There were exceptions. I do not wish to view the past through 'rose-tinted spectacles'. There were other styles of clothing worn at social occasions in Victorian and Edwardian times that were considered to be sensual. However, a remarkable fact of history greatly impressed me recently. A brother in Christ lent me a copy of a book recording the author's first-hand account of the Welsh Revival of 1904-1905. One outcome of the revival stated by the author was that many young women, who were converted to Christ during the revival, took their 'dancing frocks' which they had previously worn to balls, and destroyed them by cutting them in pieces. Their reason for doing this was that they did not wish to give in to the enticing allurements of fleshly lusts by wearing such clothing. Neither did they wish to attend balls where the temptations of the flesh would quench their love and zeal for Jesus Christ. What a challenge this example is for believers today.

However, in spite of how radically different society was, morally speaking, at that time, certain individuals pushed the boundaries. For example, I recently viewed a display on the early history of the motor car at the Ulster Folk and Transport Museum. One of the articles of writing that accompanied the photographs, stated that certain women who travelled as passengers in the early motor cars of the 1900s, claimed that they found their long skirts awkward and unsuitable for traveling in a motor car. Their solution, therefore, was to wear skirts that were shortened to the knee, with 'high' laced boots. This caused great shock in some quarters of society, since such styles were revolutionary at that time, and were not considered to be decent or modest.

But consider how much further the boundaries had been pushed by the 1920s and 1930s. The Hollywood film industry brought the movies into society, complete with glamorous actors and actresses. Ginger Rogers, and many other 'dancing' actresses appeared on screen wearing seductive silk evening dresses with the back exposed, or even outfits that resembled bathing costumes, and shoes with high heels. It is for this reason that I could never again justify watching old 'black and white' Hollywood movies for entertainment, let alone modern secular films. In their own way, actresses such as Joan Crawford, Katherine Hepburn, Ginger Rogers and many others (most of whom had multiple marriages and affairs) were just as immodest and indecent as the actresses of today. Indeed, these early female film stars helped to pave the way for the gross immodesty that would follow just a few decades later, in the hedonistic culture of the 1960s.

Following the Second World War, a 'baby boom' generation of young people grew up into a post-war liberated culture of pleasure seeking. Rock and pop musicians performed their fleshly, carnal music and promoted every form of licentiousness imaginable. *The Beatles,* for example, promoted drug abuse, Hinduism, and 'free love' (*Music For Good Or Evil,* DVD sermon series, David W. Cloud, Way of Life Literature, 2010). It was during this cultural revolution that the mini- skirt arrived on the scene. I have not seen any photographs or images of the mini-skirt as part of my research for this book. But I know that the design of this skirt was so short that it exposed the entire thighs and barely covered the posterior. That is a documented fact, and, I presume, the reason why critics have called it an 'icon' of fashion history. By this stage, immodesty had reached a pinnacle. No longer was indecency kept 'behind closed doors'; now it was, and still is today, everywhere to be seen in society. The church is no exception.

Every single style of immodest clothing that I have mentioned so far, from the most subtle forms to the very worst forms, I have witnessed being worn by professing Christian women. It is for this reason that I have found it necessary to mention virtually everything that comes to my remembrance, because very often there is nothing to distinguish between Christians and the world. If the world's standard of dress is the very opposite of **'modest',** and yet the Word of God commands **'modest apparel',** then sadly, many Christian women are failing to obey the Word of God. Not only are Christian women failing, but men who have the responsibility of teaching churches and assemblies, and their families, are failing when they avoid the subject of modesty for fear of causing offence.

I earnestly plead with the Christian woman who is reading this. Most probably, you have worn at least one of the various styles of clothing previously mentioned. It is very likely that you own some or even all of the items of clothing that I have mentioned, and perhaps others that I have not mentioned. I am absolutely convinced that according to God's standards revealed in the Bible, **not one of these styles of clothing is the 'modest apparel' that God commands.** Please read the Scriptures for yourself, and weigh up these items of clothing against what the Bible teaches. I guarantee that if you are genuine and sincere in your desire to honour Christ with your clothing, you will find that all of the afore-mentioned dress styles are **'weighed and found wanting.'**

The effect and consequences of immodesty:

"For at the window of my house I looked through my casement, and beheld among the simple ones, I discerned among the youths, a young man void of understanding, passing through the street near her corner; and he went the way to her house, in the twilight, in the evening, in the black and dark night: and behold, there met him a woman with the attire of an harlot, and subtil of heart."

Proverbs 7:6-10

Everything that we read about this woman in Proverbs chapter 7, is the opposite of the godly, modest woman described in 1 Timothy chapter 2. However, notice that **the very first aspect of this woman that the Bible describes is her manner of dress.** This is no co-incidence. This woman's clothing (or lack of clothing as the case may well have been) instantly caught the young man's attention. *This proves what other Scriptures teach also, that men are easily tempted, sexually, by what they see.* We covered this in the men's chapter earlier, and saw, particularly, that Christ's command concerning looking at a woman to lust after her (Matthew 5:28), proves this lesson. And we saw also, that it is the man's responsibility **first, to ensure that he walks in obedience to the Lord's teaching, and turns his eyes away from anything that would cause him to lust.**

When confronted with the issue of modest apparel, some Christian women, who are accustomed to dressing in a sensual fashion, respond by claiming that it is the man's fault if he has a problem with their manner of dress. They often claim that the man has a personal problem if he cannot control his eyes. By doing this, they absolve themselves from all responsibility and ignore the Bible's plain teaching. Just as the man is responsible for his eyes, the woman is equally responsible to dress and behave modestly, because the Scriptures teach these principles in no uncertain terms. It is true that if a man looks lustfully at a woman because she is dressed immodestly, he has sinned. However, the Christian woman has also sinned because she has disobeyed the clear command of Scripture to dress and behave modestly. By doing so, she has accomplished two things:

Just as the woman in Proverbs chapter 7 was identified with the evil trade of harlotry (prostitution) by her manner of dress, the Christian woman associates herself with sinful conduct by wearing immodest or indecent clothing.

Just as the woman in Proverbs chapter 7 ensnared the young man when he met her because of her manner of dress and behaviour, the Christian woman, by wearing immodest and provocative clothing, causes her Christian brother(s) to stumble.

Romans 14:21 declares: ***"It is good neither to eat flesh, nor to drink wine, nor anything whereby thy brother stumbleth, or is offended, or is made weak."*** Notice the word 'anything'. The context of Romans chapter 14 is to avoid causing offence to other believers on matters such as food and drink, and to help weaker believers not to stumble. But the word 'anything' here indicates that we can rightly apply this teaching to anything else, including the issue of dress. Consider what takes place when a Christian woman dresses in an immodest and inappropriate fashion. She causes all three things mentioned in this verse to happen. She causes her brother to stumble, and to be offended, and to be made weak. His ability to resist the temptation to lust is damaged.

The immodest and provocative dress styles mentioned in the previous chapters are often accompanied by provocative and flirtatious behaviour. It is not uncommon, even among Christians, for such a combination to lead to fornication.

That is exactly what happened to the young man in Proverbs 7. He was already 'void of understanding' (v.7) before the woman appeared, therefore he was easy prey for the devil's trap when he met her. We have already dealt with 'everyday' common items of immodest fashion clothing worn by women today. We could rightly categorise many of these as *'the attire of an harlot'*, but this woman's manner of dress could be described as the very worst form of immodest and indecent clothing imaginable. It was the clothing of a prostitute. We need not enter into great detail as we have covered enough detail in the previous chapters of this section. But we might say that this woman's clothing would have taken immodesty to an absolute extreme.

I have heard testimonies from men involved in outreach activities on weekend evenings, who seek to share the gospel with young people on the streets as they enter and leave public bars and nightclubs. One of these men, a Baptist pastor, testified that the young women who attend such places are dressed with 'hardly any clothes on at all.' This may sound like an exaggeration, but it gives us an idea of the extent of immodesty on our streets today. It is serious enough during daylight hours. How much worse it is late at night in the vicinity of the dens of iniquity in towns and cities, cannot be underestimated. Neither can it be ignored when driving at night through a town or city that happens to be popular for nightlife. I have recently found it necessary to plan any night-time journeys by car very carefully, to avoid seeing this.

On one occasion, on a summer evening, I was present at an open air gospel outreach service in a seaside town, directly opposite the entrance to a public bar or night spot of some kind. I was compelled to divert my eyes instantly away from a young woman who was standing outside this venue, because she was dressed in an outfit that resembled nothing more than underwear. Women, who dress in such a wicked and sexually provocative manner that amounts to semi-nakedness, and in full view of the public eye, are most certainly not innocent. I do hope that this young woman heard the proclamation of the gospel, and her need of salvation. Most assuredly, God loves her and gave His Son to die for her. But that does not absolve her guilt unless she repents, turns to Jesus Christ, receives forgiveness of sins, and is born again. Unless conversion takes place, and the blood of Christ is applied, there is no innocence in the sight of God. And women who deliberately dress in this manner ought to expect the evil consequences.

The example of the woman in Proverbs chapter 7 proves this lack of innocence. After describing her outward appearance in v.10, the Bible tells us that she was *'subtil of heart'.* She was crafty, cunning, manipulative and deceptive. However, these motives were not immediately apparent on the outside. They were hidden, because the young man could not see into her heart. He could only see what was on the outside. If the young man was aware of the intents and motives of this woman's heart he might have made every effort to escape immediately. **But he did not, because he was captivated, initially, by her appearance.** And the woman not only used her seductive behaviour, but used the power of her prostitute's clothing to her advantage with this young man. What is even more remarkable is that nothing else is mentioned concerning this woman's appearance, other than her manner of dress. This is in contrast to other women in the Scriptures. Consider Rebekah, for example, who is described as follows: *"And the damsel was very fair to look upon, a virgin.."* (Genesis 24:16)

Notice the difference. With Rebekah, who was to become Isaac's wife, her natural feminine beauty is emphasised, and she was pure, chaste, and innocent. Abraham's servant was able to behold her innocently, and admire her beauty without sinning, because there was nothing immodest about Rebekah's appearance. But with the woman of Proverbs chapter 7, **no natural beauty is mentioned. The power of her attraction was first and foremost, in her manner of dress.** In addition to this, her subsequent behaviour was equally seductive. Consider the description that follows, in verse 11:

> *'(She is loud and stubborn; her feet abide not in her house: now is she without, now in the streets, and lieth in wait at every corner.)'*

This behaviour is the very opposite of that described in New Testament passages that relate to Christian women's behaviour. Instead of the **'discreet'** and **'chaste'** women that we find in Titus 2:5, the woman of Proverbs chapter 7 is *"loud and stubborn"* and *"her feet abide not in her house".* The verses that follow describe how the dress and behaviour of this woman enabled her success in seducing the young man to commit adultery with her. In fact, her manner of dress and behaviour gave her the power to force him to yield to her evil intentions. This proves to us how powerful the immodest manner of a woman's dress can be in the realm of sexual temptation. Consider how the chapter concludes:

"Let not thine heart decline to her ways, go not astray in her paths. For she hath cast down many wounded: yea, many strong men have been slain by her. Her house is the way to hell, going down to the chambers of death."

Proverbs 7:25-27

The Word of God makes no mincing of words in warning men of this grave danger. We quoted earlier from a message preached by the famous Ulster evangelist, W. P. Nicholson, in 1929. Consider the following experience that he related during the same message:

"I was in London some time ago, conducting a mission there in Dr. Holden's church. A couple of society girls were converted. One night the vicar and I were going home, and those girls said to us, as we passed out of the church, "We're going the same way as you; we'll walk along with you." I turned to them and said, "You can go with the vicar if you like, but not with me." One of them looked surprised and said, "Why?" I said, "I wouldn't walk down Baker Street with you. I have a reputation to maintain, and I mean to maintain it." I said, "Why, look at yourselves in the glass. If anybody from Scotland met you with me he would say, 'Nicholson is off with a loose woman.'" She looked disgusted, and said, "Do you know this is one of the latest creations from Paris?" "No, ma'am, said I, "It's from hell; and when you dress in modesty a man might be safe in walking with you." But, my, how many there are today talking about being followers of the Lord Jesus Christ, and yet keeping to the example of the harlots of the world!" (Sermons by W.P. Nicholson, p.155-156)

How astounding it is, to consider that this message was delivered over eighty years ago. Mr. Nicholson, and other well-known gospel preachers of the last century, such as Mr. Frank Knox, were renowned for their outspoken

77

and forth-right preaching. Many were offended at their fearless denunciations of worldliness. Yet, in spite of this, these men were greatly used by God, and had the joy of seeing thousands of people come to repentance and saving faith in Jesus Christ under their ministry. If Mr. Nicholson declared some of the dress styles of the 1920s to be 'from hell', what would he say of many of the dress styles of the 21st century?

Consider the following description in Proverbs chapter 5:

> *"For the lips of a strange woman drop as an honeycomb, and her mouth is smoother than oil: but her end is bitter as wormwood, sharp as a two-edged sword. Her feet go down to death; her steps take hold on hell."*

> *Proverbs 5:3-5*

Notice how similar the woman in Proverbs chapter 5 is to the woman of Proverbs chapter 7:

> *"With her much fair speech she caused him to yield, with the flattering of her lips she forced him. He goeth after her straightway, as an ox goeth to the slaughter, or as a fool to the correction of the stocks; till a dart strike through his liver; as a bird hasteth to the snare, and knoweth not that it is for his life."*

> *Proverbs 7:21-23*

The description of the woman in Proverbs chapter 7 begins with **"the attire of an harlot"** (v.10), and concludes in v.27: *"Her house is the way to hell, going down to the chambers of death."* This proves to us that the road to hell for many men is lust, and, in this case, it began with the eyes. It reminds us of the severe warning of James:

> *"But every man is tempted, when he is drawn away of his own lust, and is enticed. Then when lust hath conceived, it bringeth forth sin: and sin, when it is finished, bringeth forth death. Do not err, my beloved brethren."*
>
> *James 1:14-16*

This reinforces the man's responsibility not to yield to temptation in the first place. However, remember that in this case, the woman was equally guilty because she deliberately approached the young man and took advantage of him. **The very first aspect that provoked the man to lust and fall into sin was the woman's manner of dress.**

Today, many Christian women, by following worldly fashion, are showing little difference between themselves and the world, when they wear items that can only be described as *'the attire of an harlot.'*

I earnestly entreat Christian women who may be reading this study, to consider their ways before God. The very fact that modesty of dress and behaviour is clearly taught in the New Testament, shows us that it was necessary for the apostles, under inspiration of the Holy Spirit, to teach women that they were not to follow the immodest worldly fashions of their contemporary culture. It is no different for us today.

THE HEART OF TRUE BIBLICAL MODESTY

I t would be extremely unfair to Christian women if I were to ignore the positive Biblical antidote to all of the previous studies on the subject of immodesty. We have already studied the principle teaching of modesty in 1 Timothy 2:9-10. The following two passages from the New Testament re-emphasise the fundamental doctrinal importance of Biblical modesty, **but also prove that true modesty begins in the heart**. When the heart is first addressed, the outward modesty of appearance ought to follow, and should reflect the condition of the heart towards God. Understanding this is essential for the spiritual help and direction of the Christian woman who is genuinely seeking God's will with regard to choosing dress styles which are modest. Consider the first of these passages:

> *"Whose adorning let it not be that outward adorning of plaiting the hair, and of wearing of gold, or of putting on of apparel; but let it be the hidden man of the heart, in that which is not corruptible, even the ornament of a meek and quiet spirit, which is in the sight of God of great price."*
>
> *1 Peter 3:3-4*

It is clear from this passage in 1 Peter, that **it is not that which is on the outside which draws attention to the Christian woman, but that which is on the inside.** Her heart cannot be seen by others. However, if she loves Jesus Christ and is devoted to His service, this will be reflected on the outside. Any immodest dress styles would contradict this testimony. For the Christian woman, it is *"the ornament of a meek and quiet spirit"* which draws attention to her spiritual character, and *"is in the sight of God of great price"*. This is a tremendous truth. No higher value could be placed upon anything that is of great price in God's sight, and here we see that a God-fearing woman's meek and quiet spirit is so valued by God. This is the inner adornment of a godly woman. Anything that is worldly or sensual, or anything that would draw inappropriate attention to her physical appearance, would cast doubt upon her devotion to Christ.

This does not suggest, in any way, that the Christian woman is to neglect her appearance, or to appear drab and unattractive. The Bible does not advocate such extremes in order to be modest. The Bible teaches in 1 Corinthians chapter 11 that *"the woman is the glory of the man"* (1 Corinthians 11:7), and *"if a woman have long hair, it is a glory to her"* (1 Corinthians 11:15). The Scriptures have never ignored the beauty of some of the women of the Old Testament who were instrumental in God's purposes, such as Sarah, Rebekah, Esther, and others, but made specific mention of their fairness. This, I believe, is a testament to the beauty of God's creation. God intended for the woman to have such loveliness, and she was created for the man (1 Corinthians 11:9). When God created the woman as a 'help-meet' for Adam, Adam declared that *"this is now bone of my bones, and flesh of my flesh: she shall be called Woman, because she was taken out of Man."* (Genesis 2:23)

For a man to appreciate the beauty of his wife is not a sin. It is right and pure. And for a woman to take care of her appearance is not a sin, nor is it disobedience to any of the passages we have examined. Indeed, the Christian woman can dress in a manner that is lovely and beautiful, but which is entirely modest and decent. She can dress in a manner that reflects both her love for Christ and her femininity, but which does not reveal or draw attention to her body which is reserved for the privacy of marriage and for her husband.

Long, loose fitting dresses and upper garments which cover the whole body properly, can be elegant, feminine, attractive and modest. Footwear with soles that do not make a loud noise when the woman walks, and which do not elevate her stature in a sensual and provocative fashion, can be just as elegant and pretty as any other item. I am not advocating a 'uniform' for Christian women. I am merely giving examples of clothing which are not suggestive or immodest. Because the vast majority of high street fashion clothing is highly immodest, it will require some effort and careful searching on the part of the Christian woman to find sources of modest clothing.

On the subject of dresses, I wish to give a word of caution with regard to some of the long, 'flowing' styles of summer dresses that are very much in vogue at the time of writing. Although these may reach almost to the ground in length, some of these dresses are very revealing above the waist, exposing a large proportion of the back and / or the bosom. Some are also made from very thin material and pose a real danger if light happens to shine through them. An additional garment worn underneath or above may render these more decent.

I wish to give a warning, also, at this point, with regard to ladies' clothing that may be 'modest' in their eyes but which is **excessively expensive.** In 1 Timothy 2:9, when the apostle Paul teaches that women adorn themselves in **'modest apparel',** the Scripture states, in the same verse, that it should not be **'costly array'.** Some may respond, "how costly is costly?" Indeed, some may argue that this is a 'relative' teaching. After all, no figure is mentioned. Most Christian women today who love their Saviour and who seek to please Him in all things will have some understanding of what is excessively expensive. Indeed, an outfit may not be indecent or suggestive, but if it costs a small fortune to purchase, it may be very ostentatious. In short, if it is extremely expensive, it will probably look extremely expensive. 'Modest apparel' and 'costly array' are two distinctly opposite attributes in 1 Timothy 2:9. If the outfit is highly ostentatious, it could not be described as 'modest'.

However, good quality clothing that is modest, may well be more expensive than the average high street store's clothing. I do not wish to enforce a specific rule, but merely wish to apply the Bible's clear teaching in a practical manner. I believe that with wisdom and discretion, the Christian woman can find good quality clothing which is modest and will last for a good period of time, at a reasonable price. If she is married, her husband, of course should be consulted at all times as her head. If he considers something to be inappropriate, immodest, or too expensive, he should decline to give his wife permission to purchase it. He should also do likewise with his daughters. This is to be done in love, and the wife is to be subject to her husband in all things as unto Christ, as clearly taught in Ephesians chapter 5.

The second passage that relates specifically to this subject is as follows:

> *"But speak thou the things that become sound doctrine: that the aged men be sober, grave, temperate, sound in faith, in charity, in patience. The aged women likewise, that they be in behaviour as becometh holiness, not false accusers, not given to much wine, teachers of good things; THAT THEY MAY TEACH THE YOUNG WOMEN TO BE SOBER, TO LOVE THEIR HUSBANDS, TO LOVE THEIR CHILDREN, TO BE DISCREET, CHASTE, KEEPERS AT HOME, GOOD,*

OBEDIENT TO THEIR OWN HUSBANDS, THAT THE WORD OF GOD BE NOT BLASPHEMED."

Titus 2:1-5

The first important truth that we learn from this passage is that the issues addressed here are *"the things that become sound doctrine"* (v.1). This refutes any argument that modesty, obedience of the wife to her husband, and being a keeper at home are 'secondary' doctrinal issues. They are as much a part of 'sound doctrine' as the other aspects referred to in the above verses, such as faith, charity, patience, chastity, holiness, love for the husband and children, etc. We have already established that the husband, as the head of the home and family, is to be the principal teacher of the Word of God to his wife and children. However, in addition to this fundamental truth, we see from Titus chapter 2 that the older women in the church are also to contribute to the spiritual maturity of young women by teaching them the fundamental principles of Biblical womanhood. And we see that they are to lead by example. They are to be *"in behaviour as becometh holiness"* and to be *"teachers of good things"* (v.3). If the older women in a church or assembly dress or behave immodestly, they will only lead the younger women astray by their poor example. If, however, they behave in holiness and teach good things, they will achieve great things for God by helping to raise up a younger generation of godly women.

Among the other things listed in this passage, the older women are to teach the younger women to be **'sober'**, **'discreet'**, **'chaste'** and **'good'**. This has a direct bearing on the subject of modesty. Compare this teaching with the same apostle's teaching in 1 Timothy 2:9-10, where Paul uses the words **'modest'**, **'shamefacedness'**, **'sobriety'**, **'godliness'**, and **'good works'**.

We do not need to be scholars of New Testament Greek to see clearly that the words used by the apostle Paul in both 1 Timothy chapter 2 and Titus chapter 2, under Divine inspiration by the Holy Spirit, are very similar. **They leave the Christian woman in no doubt as to the godly and Christ-like attributes that should characterize her daily walk with Christ. HER MANNER OF DRESS, THEREFORE WILL BE IN KEEPING WITH THIS.**

Another fundamental truth that is absolutely clear from verse 5 of this passage is this: **the godly attributes of womanhood taught in these verses are to be followed SO THAT THE WORD OF GOD BE NOT BLASPHEMED.** What a serious charge this is. This tells us that the testimony of God's Word will be **blasphemed** and brought into disrepute by immodesty or indecency of dress or behaviour.

In 1 Peter chapter 3, after teaching wives to be in subjection to their own husbands, the Bible commands husbands:

> *"Likewise, ye husbands, dwell with them according to knowledge, giving honour unto the wife, as unto the weaker vessel, and as being heirs together of the grace of life; that your prayers be not hindered."*
>
> *1 Peter 3:7*

The husband is clearly commanded to dwell with his wife and to give honour unto her. This is in keeping with those other familiar passages of Scripture that teach husbands to love their wives. **If the Christian woman walks in obedience to the Bible's commandments to wives that they be subject, submissive and obedient to their husbands, THEY WILL**

RECEIVE GREAT HONOUR AND LOVE FROM GOD-FEARING HUSBANDS WHO LOVE AND SERVE JESUS CHRIST.

Godly and sincere men who are devoted to the service of Christ will have the greatest respect for like-minded women who seek to please their Saviour by their modesty, humility, chastity, discretion, sobriety, submission to their husbands, and every other godly attribute that we have examined in the Scriptures. **ALL OF THESE QUALITIES IN A CHRIST-CENTRED HEART WILL BE REFLECTED ON THE OUTSIDE ALSO.**

In conclusion, I earnestly exhort Christian women to pursue the attributes of true Biblical womanhood and modesty. These principles have been rejected by the society and culture in which we live, which is at enmity with God.

If you are determined to seek the will of God for your life, and to be obedient to His commandments, this is not the way of bondage. It is the way of true liberty in Christ.

> *"Blessed are the undefiled in the way, who walk in the law of the LORD. Blessed are they that keep his testimonies, and that seek him with the whole heart."*
>
> *Psalm 119:1-2*

> *"For this is the love of God, that we keep his commandments: and his commandments are not grievous."*
>
> *1 John 5:3*

If you are truly devoted to the obedience of the Word of God, and wish to be modest, you will find that it is necessary to reject a very large proportion of modern fashion clothing for women. This may be difficult at first, and it may take some time to become accustomed to changing the entire contents of a wardrobe, but think of the eternal blessings that will result from obedience to the simple teachings of the Word of God. This is not 'legalism'. To obey the teachings that we find in the Word of God is the very least that should be expected of redeemed sinners who have been washed in the blood of Jesus Christ and saved by the grace of God. To obey the commandments of Jesus Christ as revealed in the pages of Holy Scripture is the way of true liberty, joy, and lasting peace.

CONCLUSION

"And as Moses lifted up the serpent in the wilderness, even so must the Son of Man be lifted up: that whosoever believeth in him should not perish, but have eternal life. For God so loved the world, that he gave his only begotten Son, that whosoever believeth in him should not perish, but have everlasting life."

John 3:14-16

This book will be of absolutely no value to the reader unless he or she is truly born again. Unless you are truly converted within, no outward reform will save your soul. It is of the utmost importance that, above all things, you know the gospel of Jesus Christ. It may be the case that a reader of this study is religious, respectable, perhaps even a 'professor' of Christianity, but not born again.

A remarkable thing in the above passage of Scripture that strikes us is this: one of the most famous sentences in the Bible is repeated twice. Consider:

"....that whosoever believeth in him should not perish but have eternal life."

John 3:15

"....that whosoever believeth in him should not perish but have everlasting life."

John 3:16

Any time a word, phrase, or sentence is repeated in Scripture, it is for the purpose of emphasis. When Jesus repeated this glorious and wonderful truth to the man Nicodemus, He did so in order to impress it deeply upon the mind and heart of this man.

The Lord Jesus did not want Nicodemus to miss that all important truth, that whosoever believes in Jesus Christ should not perish but have everlasting life. In verse 15, He used the word eternal, and in verse 16, He used the word everlasting. That is the only difference. Both words have exactly the same meaning.

The fundamental truth of these verses is that only faith in Christ can assure us of everlasting life. Nicodemus was a religious and very well-respected man in Jewish society, but when he met the Son of God he was confronted with the truth that *"...except a man be born again, he cannot see the kingdom of God."* (John 3:3)

In the conversation that followed, Jesus left Nicodemus in no doubt that he needed to be born again. When we reach verses 14-17, we find that the new birth comes through believing in Christ alone for salvation.

Coming to Jesus Christ and trusting Him alone for salvation requires an act on your part. The Bible calls this act repentance. When Jesus first began to preach, His first message was, *"The time is fulfilled, and the kingdom of God is at hand: repent ye, and believe the gospel."* (Mark 1:15)

Why are repentance and the new birth necessary? The answer is found in John chapter 3, which tells us that, as sinners without Christ, we are already under two things: firstly, the **condemnation** of God; and, secondly, the **wrath** of God:

> *"He that believeth on him is not condemned: but he that believeth not is CONDEMNED already, because he hath not believed in the name of the only begotten Son of God."*
>
> *John 3:18*

> *"He that believeth on the Son hath everlasting life: and he that believeth not the Son shall not see life; but the WRATH of God abideth on him."*
>
> *John 3:36*

The condemnation and the wrath of God lead to only one destination: hell. In Mark chapter 9, Jesus repeatedly described hell as the fire that never shall be quenched. Elsewhere, Scripture consistently describes hell in the same manner.

No amount of good living, kind deeds or charitable acts will save you. Jesus, in His Word, makes it abundantly clear that only through repentance and faith in Him can anyone be saved and receive the promise of eternal life. If you have never trusted Him, I urge you, above all else, to do so now, that you might be saved, have peace with God, forgiveness of sins, and the promise of eternal life.

BIBLIOGRAPHY

Cloud, David W., *Dressing For the Lord,* Way of Life Literature, 2007.

Cloud, David W., *What is the Emerging Church?,* Way of Life Literature, 2009.

Kidd, David, *The Fall and Rise of Christian Standards, Thinking Biblically About Dress and Appearance,* Xulon Press, 2005.

Matthews, David, *I Saw the Welsh Revival,* Ambassador Publications, 2004.

Morton, Grenfell, *Railways in Ulster, Historic Photographs of the Age of Steam,* Friar's Bush Press, 1989.

Paisley, Ian R.K., *Sermons by W.P. Nicholson, Tornado of the Pulpit, Biographical Sketch by Ian R.K. Paisley, M.P.,* Martyrs Memorial Publications, 1982.

Schrock, Simon, *What Shall the Redeemed Wear?* Campbell Copy Center, 2000.

Strong, James, *Strong's Exhaustive Concordance of the Bible,* World Bible Publishers (date of this edition not printed in publication but *Strong's Exhaustive Concordance of the Bible* was first published in 1890).

Wigram, George V., *The Englishman's Greek Concordance of the New Testament,* Hendrickson Publishers, 1998